MONTGOMERY COLLEGE LIBRARY
GERMANTOWN CAMPUS

THE PRESIDENT AND CONGRESS

1964
1960
1956
1924
1916
1912
1920
1900
1896
1888

THE PRESIDENT AND CONGRESS

TOWARD A NEW POWER BALANCE

JAMES W. DAVIS — Western Washington State College

DELBERT RINGQUIST — Central Michigan University

Politics in Government Series
Mary Earhart Dillon, Editor

BARRON'S EDUCATIONAL SERIES, INC.   WOODBURY, NEW YORK

Acknowledgements

The editor gratefully acknowledges the aid of the U.S. Government Printing Office in locating and supplying photographs. Also acknowledged is the assistance of the House Banking and Currency Committee, U.S. Capitol Historical Society, and Mr. Arthur E. Scott, in supplying photographs.

© Copyright 1975 by Barron's Educational Series, Inc.

All rights reserved.
No part of this book may be reproduced
in any form, by photostat, microfilm, xerography,
or any other means, or incorporated into any
information retrieval system, electronic or
mechanical, without the written permission
of the copyright owner.

All inquiries should be addressed to:
Barron's Educational Series, Inc.
113 Crossways Park Drive
Woodbury, New York 11797

Library of Congress Catalog Card No. 74–26595

International Standard Book No. 0–8120–0510–4

Library of Congress Cataloging in Publication Data

Davis, James W   1920–
    The President and Congress, toward a new power balance.
    (Politics in government series)
    SUMMARY: Traces the historical relationship between the President and Congress and discusses events of the Nixon administration which indicate a shifting balance of power between those two branches of government.
    1. Separation of powers—United States. 2. Presidents—United States. 3. United States. Congress. [1. Separation of powers. 2. Presidents. 3. United States. Congress. [I. Ringquist, Delbert, joint author. II. Title.
JK305.D38   353.02   74–26595
ISBN 0–8120–0510–4

PRINTED IN THE UNITED STATES OF AMERICA

CONTENTS ★

Introduction   xi

1 The Setting   1
The Highwater Mark of Presidential Influence   2
His Royal Majesty—The President   4
The 'High-Flying' Presidentialists   5
Vietnam and the "Revisionist" Attack on the Presidency   7
Resurgence of Congress   9
Impact of the Watergate Affair   11
Impeachment Threat   13

2 The Presidential-Congressional See-Saw: Historical Overview   16
Framers' Intentions   16
Early Contests between Congress and President   18
Early Congressional Ascendancy   20
Lincoln: Prototype of the Modern President   23
Post-Civil War Congressional Dominance   25
The Presidency Comes of Age: TR to FDR   28
The New Deal Era—The White House Takes Over   32
Congressional Eclipse in the Modern Era   35
Conclusion   38

3 Presidential Versus Congressional Leadership   40
Presidentialists Versus Congressionalists   40
Theories of Leadership   43
Dual System of Representation   45
White House Leadership Models   47
The President as Persuader   52
The View from Capitol Hill   54
Congress: Tribune of the People?   56

Presidential-Congressional Deadlock?	58
Two Presidencies	59
Shared Leadership	65

4 Uneasy Partners: Congress and the President in Foreign Affairs — 67

Constitutional Division	68
The Treaty-Making Powers	70
Executive Agreements	75
Congressional Efforts to Curtail Executive Usurpation	79

5 Commander-in-Chief or Congress: Who Makes War? — 81

Conflicting Theories of War-Making Powers	81
Madison View	83
Polk View	84
Lyndon Johnson View	84
Presidential Interventionism	85
National Emergencies	87
Presidential Advantages: Real or Imagined?	88
Congressional Actions to Curb War-Making Power	91
Unfinished Business	93
Public Support of Presidents during Wartime	94

6 President and Congress: Who Controls the Direction of Domestic Policy? — 96

Legislative Powers	96
Veto Power	97
Informal Presidential Power	99
President: The Great Initiator	102
Presidential Messages	103
White House Lobbying on Capitol Hill	104
Congressional Legislative Machinery	107
Congressional Delegation of Power	111
Impoundment	113
Congressional Follow-up and Oversight	115
Executive Privilege	115

Contents

Appointment and Oversight	118
Investigation	121
Legislative Veto	123
Conclusion	123

7 Cooperation Between Executive and Legislative Branches — 125

Meeting Each Other Halfway	125
Role of Party	126
International and Domestic Crises	128
Cooperation: Part-Time Only	129
Proposals to Improve Presidential-Congressional Cooperation	133
Critique of Proposed Reforms	140
What Is to Be Done?	142

8 Effect of Watergate and Impeachment Threat on Presidential-Congressional Relations — 147

Switch in Presidential Posture	147
Congressional Renaissance	148
Growing Threat of Impeachment against President Nixon	151
Impeachment: The Ultimate Check	152
The Nixon Impeachment Inquiry	156
The President's Diminishing Options	160
Nixon Yields to Congress on Other Fronts	165

9 Toward a New Political Order — 166

The Dilemma of Power	167
Lessons of Watergate, the Impeachment Inquiry, and the Nixon Resignation	169
Nixon's Unconditional Pardon Ends New President's Political "Honeymoon"	170
FOOTNOTES	175
TOPICS FOR PAPERS OR ORAL REPORTS	190
BIBLIOGRAPHY	196
INDEX	200

TITLES IN THIS SERIES

Published

THE CORPORATIONS AND SOCIAL CHANGE

DOES THE CITIZEN STAND A CHANCE?
  Politics of a State Legislature: New York

NATIONAL CONVENTIONS:
  Nominations Under the Big Top

THE POLITICS OF PEOPLE-POWER:
  Interest Groups and Lobbies in New York State

THE POLITICS OF URBANISM:
  The New Federalism

PRESSURES UPON CONGRESS:
  Legislation by Lobby

THE PRESIDENT AND CONGRESS:
  Toward a New Power Balance

In Preparation

ALTERNATIVE FUTURES:
  Political Choices for Tomorrow

BLACK POWER IN DIXIE:
  The Politics of the Ghetto

BLACK WOMEN:
  Their Problems and Power

THE POLITICS OF BUREAUCRACY

POLITICS OF CONGRESSIONAL COMMITTEES:
  The Power of Seniority

FAMILY, VILLAGE AND FACTORY:
  Ordinary Life in the New China

THE FUTURE OF FAMILY:
  Love, Sex, Marriage, No Children

THE POLITICS OF INTERNATIONAL RELATIONS:
  The Middle East and World Affairs

THE POLITICS OF JAPAN:
  Government and Business—A Successful Marriage

LATIN AMERICA IN WORLD AFFAIRS:
The Politics of Inequality

PENTAGON POLITICS:
The Clash with Civilian Reality

THE PERSIAN GULF REGION AND THE WORLD:
Oil and Politics

THE WINNING OF THE PRESIDENCY:
The Difficulty of Elections

THE MYSTIQUE OF THE PRESIDENT:
Politics and Power

THE POLITICS OF RELIGION:
An Institution in Crisis

THE TANGLED FINANCES OF THE CITY OF NEW YORK:
The Urban Budget

UNEMPLOYMENT:
The Problem of Prosperity

VIOLENCE:
The Social-Psychological Pressures and Some Solutions

WALL STREET AND AMERICA

General Editor: Mary Earhart Dillon, formerly Chairman of the Department of Political Science, Queens College of the City University of New York

INTRODUCTION ★

The Politics of Government Series is a continuing publication of paperbacks written by recognized scholars on conflicting issues of this disturbed society. The authors assess fast moving events and are au courant with the problems in Washington, Cairo, Damascus and Tel Aviv. These small books are especially valuable to students for the clarity of the discussion, academic accuracy, simplicity of language, excellent bibliography of recent books and a list of several hundred titles for easy selection of subject for superior class reports.

The President and Congress: Towards a New Power Balance by James W. Davis and Delbert Ringquist is a well told account of the struggle for power between the Congress and the President from the beginning of the Republic to the tragic collapse of the Nixon Administration.

George Washington was a strong President and made important decisions of procedure as well as substance such as the single visit he made to the Senate to seek "advice and consent" of his first treaty—an Indian agreement. The coolness of his reception so annoyed him he swiftly left the Chamber never to return. Thereafter, treaties were sent by messenger to the Secretary of the upper House for discussion and vote by that body only *after* negotiations were concluded. This procedure has been followed ever since.

The power of the presidency grew spasmodically gaining ground when strong presidents were in office and losing under weak presidents. After Washington and Jefferson, three weak executives followed and Congress gloried in its undisputed strength. But under Andrew Jackson (1829–1837), presidential control grew rapidly so that the press and cartoons of the day labelled him "King Andy." The Whig Party was formed in opposition to him (1834) to try to restore to Congress its damaged image.

Probably just as important in the accretion of authority to the presidency, however, was the continued weakness of Congress itself. Over the years, the legislature failed to develop stable leadership and direction. It remains a sprawling, conglomerate body with an inefficient, confused system of committees under chairmen of seniority although slightly modified in January 1975. Until Congress can reform itself and establish responsible leadership it could hardly assume any major executive power in this disjointed world.

In this technological age when decisions must be made promptly and when the government must negotiate with totalitarian regimes such as the USSR that can maneuver with ease and agility it has become apparent that only the President can function with the needed flexibility.

In 1974, *Watergate* became the symbol of the long rivalry between the sovereign powers of Congress and the Executive Powers of the President. The one charged "abuse of powers" and the other defended with the traditional rights of "Executive Privilege."

The authors are well known in the field of Government and have published books and articles. They have given a balanced and just discussion of this complex constitutional issue although tilting the scale a little in favor of more power for the Congress.

Dr. Davis is professor of Political Science and Dean of the College of Arts and Sciences at Western Washington State College and Dr. Delbert Ringquist is Professor of Political Science and Chairman of the Department at Central Michigan University.

M.E.D.

PREFACE ★

This study is not another of the "revisionist" attacks upon the strong presidency and the New Deal-Great Society liberalism that have been appearing recently with growing frequency. Nor is this study of the President and Congress either "pro-President" or "pro-Congress." Rather it is a realistic attempt to describe and assess the dynamics of White House-congressional interaction as we move toward the last quarter of the twentieth century.

It will be our goal to analyze and assess the long-term and sometimes turbulent relations between the chief executive and Congress and to explore ways of achieving accountability without paralyzing the presidency. In recent years there have been recurring complaints that Presidents have, in Thomas Cronin's words, "become very like empeor-kings, dominating public communication, determining national priorities and removing themselves from criticism and even, sometimes, from public protest." The founding fathers placed great faith in the doctrine of self-restraint to keep each branch of government from interfering too much in the responsibilities of the other branches. Checks and balances were supposed to operate automatically, but they have not.

During most of the twentieth century the power of the presidency has continued to expand at the expense of Congress and the American people. Presidents have forgotten about self-restraint or have deliberately ignored this precept. Unfortunately, in the past two decades congressional power of the purse has fallen to an all-time low, leaving the President broad latitude to carry on his executive duties with minimal congressional oversight. And since the early days of the twentieth century, when President Theodore Roosevelt "took" Panama from Colombia, the White House has operated with virtually "blank-check" authority in foreign affairs. When foreign adventures have proved disastrous, or have risked war, the President has been criticized. But he has not been censured, nor—until 1974—has he been subjected to impeachment proceedings.

Presidents Lyndon B. Johnson and Richard M. Nixon appear to have overestimated the willingness of Congress and the American electorate to tolerate the excessive use of presidential power to achieve foreign and domestic objectives—as defined by these chief executives. By coincidence both of these Presidents won huge landslide electoral victories over weak opponents—a 16-million vote margin for Mr. Johnson and an 18-million one for Mr. Nixon. Subsequently, however, both of these men overplayed their hands. President Johnson thought that he could settle the Vietnam civil war by ordering the massive intervention of 525,000 American troops into the jungles of Indochina. He failed. Recognizing his mistake too late, President Johnson halted further escalation of the war by American troops early in the spring of 1968. However, by then the massive internal divisions and antiwar protests within the country, especially among young people, forced him to withdraw from the election race in 1968. President Nixon, intoxicated with the power and prestige that White House occupancy brings, apparently concluded that he did not have to abide by the same rule of law to which all other citizens must adhere. His failure to accept this guiding principle when he approved the establishment of the unauthorized White House "plumbers" investigating unit and his basically cavalier attitude toward Congress and the checks and balances system brought him, in the summer of 1974, to political destruction—the first President in our 185-year history to be driven from office.

The 1973 Senate Watergate Committee investigation of the White House involvement in the break-in of the Democratic National Committee headquarters and the subsequent cover-up activities alerted the American public to the potential abuses of an unreined chief executive. Far more important, however, the threatened impeachment of President Nixon has focused, as no other event of the twentieth century has, on the need for the constitutional safeguards provided by the ponderous yet delicate system of checks and balances designed by the founding fathers. Though some critics have charged that Congress and the courts operate long after the fact—often too late—to check and balance executive authority, the historic events of 1974 have convincingly demonstrated that the system has worked almost exactly as the architects of the Constitution contemplated "to prevent the chief executive from engaging in the gross abuse of the tremendous power invested in that office."

It is our view that a shift in the balance of power between the President and Congress became evident soon after the second Nixon inauguration in January, 1973. The precipitating elements stemmed from two developments: (1) President Nixon's impoundment and refusal to spend for budgetary reasons more than $12 billion (some critics placed it closer to $16 billion) of congressional appropriated funds during fiscal years 1972 and 1973; and (2) Mr. Nixon's unilateral decisions to mine the harbor and waters near Haiphong, North Vietnam, in May, 1972, and to unleash without any congressional consultation the massive B-52 bombings of North Vietnamese cities over the Christmas holidays in December, 1972—a decision that provoked almost universal condemnation in Western countries. Further, it is our judgment that a redistribution of power between the White House and Capitol Hill would probably have occurred even without the Watergate scandals and the impeachment inquiry against President Nixon. But these observations take us far ahead of the main story, which is to explain to the reader how the President and Congress function in our unique separation of powers system.

In the pages that follow we will also endeavor to show that the American system operates most effectively when the President and Congress share decision making. Indeed, history shows a relatively high degree of presidential-congressional interdependence over the years. Congress has been an instrumental and durable partner in initiating and pushing through both houses much social-action legislation. We concur with David Price that instigation and formulation of new legislation needs to be a widely shared function. While executive resources are often superior, Congress has often displayed greater flexibility in molding the legislation into final form. Several case studies show that congressmen have frequently been more successful than the executive branch in generating public interest in new legislative proposals. For example, the Tennessee Valley Authority was sponsored originally by Senator George Norris of Nebraska and the Atomic Energy Commission was first proposed by the late Senator Brien McMahon of Connecticut. New ideas often seem to percolate to the top more slowly in the executive branch. But there was less sharing of power between the President and Congress during the Nixon Administrations than at any other time in recent memory. The prevailing White House view was that the whole government should be run from the Oval Office. This overcentralization of power in the presidency was indirectly on trial during the Nixon impeachment inquiry.

Despite President Nixon's resignation, we believe that the office of the presidency will have to be restructured and somehow brought more effectively under democratic control. Most other self-governing countries, it should be noted, have parliamentary systems in which the prime minister must carry a majority of his colleagues in the cabinet with him before making a major decision. Furthermore, these leaders are collectively responsible to the national legislature. But we do not advocate a parliamentary system for the United States. To function effectively, such systems require far more party discipline than members of the House and Senate would be willing to tolerate; nor can we envision an American President willing to share executive decision making with his congressional colleagues. Nevertheless, some changes or adjustments will have to be made in our national government if we are to avoid the "imperial presidency" and the traumatic events of 1974 that have produced the greatest crisis in the presidency in 107 years.

In our concluding chapters we discuss some proposals for "reining in" the President and for making Congress a more responsible coequal branch of government.

THE SETTING

The scene was the Oval Office of the White House. The date was January 29, 1973. President Nixon had just announced his proposed fiscal 1974 federal budget that he had forwarded to Capitol Hill. His new budget urged a sharp pruning of federal social programs that, in effect, would repeal the major social welfare initiatives of the Truman, Eisenhower, Kennedy, and Johnson administrations. So confident was Mr. Nixon, in light of his 1972 election, that he proposed without hesitation the curtailment or dismantling of 100 New Deal-Fair Deal-New Frontier-Great Society programs without a by-your-leave from Congress.

This was his second message to the new 93rd Congress. Earlier in the month the President had dispatched a copy of his State of the Union address to Capitol Hill to be read to the senators and house members by congressional clerks. Traditionally, Presidents since Woodrow Wilson had delivered the State of the Union message in person to the assembled lawmakers. But President Nixon, barely disguising his low regard for the recent performances of the senators and representatives—especially those of the Democratic majorities in both houses—decided not to travel to Capitol Hill.[1] The power fulcrum in Washington, he wished to emphasize, was located behind the iron gates at 1600 Pennsylvania Avenue. This was the third presidential put-down of the lawmakers since they had convened at the beginning of January. On the opening day the White House, in an unmistakable power play to downgrade the returning solons, had announced a wholesale reorganization of the executive branch by executive order, since Congress had refused to approve an earlier reorganization plan. Impatient with the separation of powers doctrine, President Nixon proposed to centralize power in the White House. Henceforth, in the words of one panel of public administration specialists, Mr. Nixon planned that:

The U.S. Government would be run like a corporation—or at least a popular view of the corporate model—with all powers concentrated at the top and exercised through appointees in the President's office and loyal followers throughout the executive branch.[2]

How near the American government would be to this closed hierarchical model today had not the Watergate scandals and Mr. Nixon's threatened impeachment halted this centralized trend, no one can say. But in the opening weeks of his second term President Nixon was obviously determined to reshape the federal government according to his own specifications. He elevated his principal assistants, for example H. R. Haldeman and John Ehrlichman, into "assistant Presidents." To achieve maximum White House control over the federal bureaucracy and to prevent Congress from exercising its traditional oversight function, such as questioning cabinet officers before congressional committees, President Nixon interposed these administrative assistants between himself and the regular executive departments. As White House aides, these officers did not have to testify on Capitol Hill. He also transformed the Office of Management and Budget, a staff agency, into the general manager of the executive branch.

Mr. Nixon had another reason for being supremely confident and high spirited following his second inauguration—the Vietnam cease-fire had just been negotiated.

The Highwater Mark of Presidential Influence

On January 27, 1973, the President and his dashing foreign policy expert, Henry Kissinger, proudly announced to the American public, via nationwide television, the cessation of hostilities in Vietnam and the North Vietnamese agreement to return all American POW's held by the Hanoi government. Though he may not have realized it at the time, the president was at the high tide of his popularity—according to a January, 1973, Gallup poll, 69 percent of those interviewed approved of the way President

The President and the House Minority Leader

President Johnson's "State of the Union"

"And so, my fellow Americans, ask not what your country can do for you — ask what you can do for your country."

John F. Kennedy

Nixon was handling his job. Though other recent Presidents had received higher ratings at some time during their terms, no peacetime chief executive ever proclaimed more power and authority in the name of the presidency than Mr. Nixon in the opening days of his second term. Despite the shocking revelations of clandestine White House activities made by Senator Ervin's Special Watergate Investigation Committee, President Nixon defended his right to use United States military forces secretly in the Laotian War and to carry on U.S. bombing of Cambodian rebel forces in the face of explicit disapproval by a majority of both houses of Congress. Furthermore, at the Watergate hearings, former presidential aide John Ehrlichman, coached by a lawyer with close White House ties, proclaimed an "inherent power" for the President to establish a White House Special Investigations Unit—the so-called "plumbers" group—to wiretap, spy, and commit burglaries in the name of "national security."

As late as April 30, 1973, Mr. Nixon's Secretary of State, William P. Rogers, had argued before the Senate Foreign Relations Committee that the Nixon Administration was legally justified by the Constitution to continue the American bombing in Cambodia as "a meaningful interim action" to force the Communist-backed insurgents to agree to a cease-fire—even though all American land forces had been withdrawn from Indochina.[3] Four months later—and five days after Congress had imposed a total ban on U.S. bombing in Cambodia after August 15, 1973—the President still proudly defended as "absolutely necessary" his secret bombing of Cambodia in 1969 in a speech before the National Convention of the Veterans of Foreign Wars in New Orleans. Speaking to the friendly audience of several thousand delegates, the President defiantly announced that if he had to do it over again, he would order such air strikes again "to save American lives."[4]

If President Nixon's words sounded somewhat like those of King Louis XIV, the reasons may well be found in the imperial manner and life-style to which American Presidents have become accustomed in recent years.

His Royal Majesty: The President

American Presidents now enjoy a life-style that would turn Alexander the Great or Augustus Caesar green with envy. President Nixon, according to a recent count, had reserved for his exclusive use five magnificently equipped Boeing 707 jetliners, eleven Lockheed jetstars, sixteen helicopters, a fleet of black limousines, one yacht, a cost-free White House with a domestic staff numbering in the dozens, and a rustic retreat (Camp David) in the Catoctin Mountains of Maryland. In addition, he personally owned his so-called winter White House at Key Biscayne, Florida, and his summer White House at San Clemente, California, overlooking the Pacific. The cost of government improvements for "security reasons" on these two residences exceeded $10 million. Until the energy crisis became a crucial issue in the midst of the 1973 Arab-Israeli October War, President Nixon flew back and forth regularly between these favorite retreats in a royal fashion that not even multimillionaires Howard Hughes or J. Paul Getty could equal. Overall, the estimated actual cost of running the presidency has been placed as high as $100 million a year.[5]

It should be pointed out that this wish to live in such regal style did not begin with President Nixon—though he probably carried it to the greatest extreme. President Johnson, his predecessor, was all too prone to speak of *my* generals, *my* aircraft, *my* helicopters, and *my* tanks. George Reedy, President Johnson's former press secretary and special assistant, has discerned a growing monarchical trend in the presidency. As Reedy put it:

> By the twentieth century the presidency had taken on all the regalia of monarchy, except ermine robes, a scepter, and a crown. The president was not to be jostled by a crowd—unless he elected to subject himself to do so during those moments when he shed his role as chief of state and mounted the hustings as a candidate for re-election. The ritual of shaking hands with the president took on more and more the coloration of the medieval "king's touch" as a specific for scrofula. The presi-

dent was not to be called to account by any other body (after the doctrine of executive privilege was established). In time another kingly habit began to appear and presidents referred to themselves more and more as "we"—the ultimate hallmark of imperial majesty.[6]

Nor have the memories of the Kennedy "court" been forgotten —especially the white-tied White House galas attended by stars of the Broadway stage, Hollywood celebrities, and champions of sport. In this brief Camelot era, world-renowned cellist Pablo Casals was invited to play for the guests, and the captains of industry mingled with the admirals and generals while the first lady set the pattern of style with her latest Paris-designed gown.

Under these circumstances, it is understandable why our recent Presidents, even those with strong egalitarian leanings, have more and more taken on the habits and life-style of reigning monarchs.

If the American presidency has, in a sense, become larger than life, part of the blame rests with liberal academicians and commentators—the so-called "presidentialists."

The 'High-Flying' Presidentialists

Standard textbooks on American government have for years given a strong endorsement to the "activist-purposeful-progressive and powerful presidency."[7] Repeatedly, American academicians have produced an exaggerated view of presidential power and capabilities. According to one team of authors, "The President is the most strategic policy-maker in the government. His policy role is paramount in military and foreign affairs."[8] Another prominent author writes:

He [John Kennedy] also became the most important and powerful chief executive in the free world. His powers are so vast that they rival those of the Soviet Premier or any other dictator. . . . He is the chief architect of the nation's public policy; as President he is one who proposes, requests, supports demands, and insists that Congress enact most of the major legislation that it does.[9]

Since the emergence of the United States as a world power at the beginning of the twentieth century, it has become a tenet of the presidentialists that a strong, independent executive is to be preferred to the fragmented leadership of Congress. Only the President, according to the presidentialists, could provide the powerful leadership to cope with continuing domestic and international crises. As the chief formulator of public policy, the President and his advisors could frontally attack the nation's problems with the maximum resources of the executive branch.

The support of ivory-towered intellectuals, of course, has not been the prime cause for the expansion of presidential power. The Great Depression, two world wars, the development of nuclear weaponry, East-West tensions reflected in the cold war, the American intervention in the Korean War, and the rise of the welfare state have all contributed to the growth of the presidency. The increasing centralization of foreign policy in the hands of the President and the expanded global defense commitments made by the United States after World War II have reinforced presidential authority and undermined Congress' ability to share in the making of public policy. For much of this century, it might be noted, the power of the legislative branch relative to the executive branch has been declining throughout the world.

The decline and fall of congressional influence over foreign policy and the war-making power have been vividly described by historian Arthur Schlesinger, Jr., who admits that while serving as one of President Kennedy's special assistants, he too helped contribute to the growth of *The Imperial Presidency*.[10] In retrospect, Schlesinger now deplores Congress' inability in the 1960's to withstand the overpowering pressure of the presidency:

> Mesmerized by the supposed need for instant response to constant crisis, overawed by what the Senate Foreign Relations Committee later called the cult of executive expertise, confused in its own mind as to what wise policy should be,

The Election Over

Two Leaders of Opposite Parties

The Setting

delighted to relinquish responsibility, Congress readily capitulated to what Corwin at the start of the fifties has called 'high-flying' theses of presidential prerogative. [11]

As late as 1965, a leading authority on the presidency, Louis Koenig, published an article glowingly entitled "More Power to the President (Not Less)." [12]

Leading spokesmen of the "Eastern Establishment" were also among the staunchest supporters of the presidency and the sharpest critics of Congress. The *Washington Post* and the *New York Times,* Schlesinger notes, "were as ardent defenders of the Presidency as anyone in the White House." [13]

Nor were conservative spokesmen any less enthusiastic about transferring the war-making power to the President. "The Constitution," said Senator Barry Goldwater, the defeated right-wing Republican presidential candidate in 1964, "gives the President, not the Congress, the primary war-making powers." [14] Senate GOP Minority Leader Everett M. Dirksen told the Senate in 1967, ". . . I have run down many legal cases before the Supreme Court . . . that I have found as yet no delimitation on the power of the Commander in Chief under the Constitution." [15] With this type of intellectual leadership it is no wonder that Congress fell further under the spell of the President during the early years of American involvement in Vietnam.

Vietnam and the "Revisionist" Attack on the Presidency

What, then, accounts for the gradual switch in congressional attitudes and public opinion concerning the presidency since the late 1960's? The United States' disastrous experience in the Vietnam War was a principal factor. Though this shift in attitudes occurred slowly in the early stages of American involvement, American disenchantment with the bloody Indochina conflict continued to grow with each passing month. United States support of South Vietnam led eventually to the dispatch of more than 500,000 troops to Southeast Asia at the peak of our involvement in 1967–68. The tragic Vietnam War caused more than 47,000 deaths among American servicemen and more than 153,000 wounded veterans. President Johnson, whose early rallying victory cry had been "bring home the coonskin," himself became one of the chief casualties of the war. The pressure of public opinion, as reflected by his low ratings in the early Gallup polls (in late 1967 only 35 percent of the respondents rated him favorably in his job performance), coupled with widespread student protests across America, and an impending defeat in the 1968 Wisconsin presidential primary, helped persuade Johnson to withdraw from his reelection nominating drive on March 31, 1968.

The Vietnam War also sent shock waves through the ranks of presidential scholars. At the height of presidential prestige and, conversely, the depth of congressional influence, the proponents of the executive dominance theory underwent a traumatic experience. As explained by one observer:

> The trauma of the [Southeast Asian] war was especially intense for the intellectual community since it was, in no small measure, their war. They had provided the foreign aid, the military and logistical theory, and much of the leadership which had made the war possible.[16]

As a result of the fruitless war in Indochina, leading presidential scholars, long champions of the President as the dynamic —almost infallible—leader in the American political system, began to have second thoughts about presidential supremacy. Several years elapsed, however, after Johnson's unilateral decision to escalate American troop involvement in Vietnam, before most presidential scholars came to realize what many other members of the intellectual community had long before concluded about the presidency—the man in the White House possessed too much untrammelled authority over the lives and the future of American citizens. These presidentialists began rereading James Madison's notes from the Constitutional Convention. The checks and balances system and the separation of pow-

The Setting

ers doctrine expounded by Madison now sounded as appealing to these scholars as they had originally to the founding fathers. The presidentialists concluded that the authors of the Constitution understood, far better than twentieth-century writers, the dangers of unchecked power. The scholars also began reassessing Congress. The legislative branch, the presidential scholars recognized, should exercise a degree of direct control over the executive branch, especially in foreign affairs and in questions relating to the war-making power.

Once fiercely critical of Congress, the former presidentialists suddenly found merit where in the past they had perceived only weakness. The congressional investigation, its importance discounted over the years, suddenly gained favor among those formerly espousing presidential dominance. Traditional conservatives, long-time proponents of dispersed power with a preference for the entrenched leadership of Congress to neutralize a strong chief executive, suddenly discovered some strange new bedfellows—the former presidentialists. The widely espoused concept of functional specialization that finds the President proposing laws and initiating public policy and Congress limited chiefly to approving and overseeing these activities, fell into disfavor.[17] Clearly, the shift of attitudes toward the President and Congress within the nation was at least as dramatic as that which occurred in the early 1930's. The dominant belief was that a redistribution of power in favor of coequally shared power between the President and Congress should take place within the national government.

Lawmakers on Capitol Hill were also engaged in some deep soul-searching.

Resurgence of Congress

By the summer of 1970 the Senate "dove" (peace) faction—mostly liberal Democrats—came within a handful of votes of cutting off funds for American involvement in the Vietnam War. Another two years passed, however, before the Senate doves succeeded in passing an "end-the-war" resolution (provided all

American POW's were returned).[18] Throughout this period, however, control of the House of Representatives remained in the hands of a "hawkish" (militant) bipartisan majority composed of southern Democrats and thick-or-thin GOP members prepared to support the Republican chief executive at every turn.

The year 1973, however, marked a major turning point in presidential-congressional relations. On January 27, 1973, the Vietnam cease-fire and prisoner of war exchange agreements were signed in Paris by President Nixon's special representative, Henry Kissinger, and the North and South Vietnamese emissaries. Majorities in both the Senate and House now felt that the United States had paid its full measure of support in American lives and money to the government of South Vietnam. The public opinion polls mirrored this overwhelming disenchantment with the war—a majority of respondents now considered American involvement in Vietnam a grave mistake. Many congressmen, too, now felt that it had been a mistake to have ever become entangled in the Vietnam quagmire. They sought to pin the blame for this error not on themselves but on President Johnson—and to a lesser extent on Presidents Kennedy and Nixon. Henceforth, lawmakers were determined that this type of presidential "blank-check" military commitment abroad would not happen again, at least not without specific authorization by a majority of both houses of Congress.

The reassertion of congressional prerogatives was also provoked by other presidential actions. President Nixon's impoundment of approximately $12 billion in funds appropriated by Congress in late 1972 for various water treatment and sewage projects, highway construction, and educational grants to the states triggered a violent reaction on Capitol Hill. Nothing is more dear to the heart of a congressman than the federal money appropriated for sewage treatment plants or other government projects in his district. These appropriations are valid proof of his influence and "clout" in Washington. For the President to seize these funds—money already appropriated and approved by both houses and the President—incensed many lawmakers, Democrats and Republicans alike. President Nixon, exuding confidence in light of his overwhelming victory in the 1972 presidential election, asserted that impoundment was necessary to keep the budget balanced, since, according to Mr. Nixon, the big spenders in Congress refused to face up to the hard reality of keeping the lid on the federal budget. Congressmen and senators (especially those of the Democratic majority) did not take this criticism lightly, and they soon turned on the President with a vengeance.

Impact of the Watergate Affair

Shortly before the battle over impoundment erupted on Capitol Hill, a special team of two investigative reporters from the *Washington Post* uncovered evidence that the Watergate "burglars" arrested in June, 1972, for the break-in at the Democratic National Committee Headquarters not only had close ties with the Committee for the Reelection of the President but also had connections that led directly to the White House.[19] From the moment Federal District Court Judge John J. Sirica imposed provisional heavy sentences on the Watergate defendants in January, 1973 (with reduced terms if they told the judge and the federal grand jury what further details they knew of the White House involvement with the break-in), President Nixon's leadership and reputation began sliding downhill—and this decline never was halted.

Sensing a major scandal in the making, the U.S. Senate voted 77 to 0—after two days of partisan debate—in February, 1973, to establish a special Watergate Investigating Committee to look into all phases of the Watergate break-in and the subsequent cover-up activities, as well as the high-priced financing of the 1972 presidential campaign.[20]

Within a ten-week period, the Watergate investigators, under the chairmanship of Senator Sam Ervin (D.-N.C.), uncovered a string of unlawful acts ranging from illegal entry to burglary, perjury, misuse of the FBI and CIA to cover up illegal activity, the destruction of evidence, the creation of a White House secret police unit (the so-called "plumbers" group) illegal wiretapping, and the existence of secret White House tapes. They also traced the tortuous and illegal path of corporate contributions and the questionable White House intervention in the International Telephone and Telegraph (ITT) antitrust and milk fund cases. This enumeration does not exhaust the list of moral calamities that involved members of the White House staff and, apparently, President Nixon himself. But one thing "is perfectly clear" since the Watergate scandal erupted: the power relationships between the President and Congress, heavily weighted in favor of the White House for more than four decades, will probably never again be so lopsided in favor of the President.

Clearly, the year 1973 marked the reemergence of Congress as a truly coequal branch of the federal government. As a result of the impoundment battle and the Watergate affair, Congress has undergone a process of revitalization. The lawmakers no longer hesitated to stand up to the President on foreign affairs or in disputes over the war-making power. By mid-summer, Congress imposed an absolute ban on the use of U.S. funds in order to halt further American bombing of rebel forces in Cambodia on August 15, 1973. Four months later, Congress quickly overrode, by more than the required two-thirds majority, a presidential veto of the War Powers Act of 1973—a measure that will curtail presidential efforts to send American troops overseas without the specific approval of both houses of Congress.

On the domestic front, Congress passed the Congressional Budget and Impoundment Control Act of 1974 to reassert legislative control over the federal budget and appropriations.[21] The new legislation empowers Congress to establish special budget committees in each house. These committees will consider all federal spending each year as a single package, clamp a ceiling on total outlays, and fix a target surplus or deficit. The budget reform legislation also establishes a special congressional budget office to provide the lawmakers with the same kind of technical data and expertise that the President receives from his Office of Management and Budget. Provisions to curtail presidential impoundment of appropriated funds are also included in the new law.

Impeachment Threat

Without doubt the Watergate affair and the subsequent White House cover-up, plus further revelations of President Nixon's alleged excessive deductions on his income tax returns, allegations of the destruction of evidence on White House tapes, and finally the house impeachment inquiry, cast the darkest shadow over the presidency since the impeachment trial of President Andrew Johnson after the Civil War.

After President Nixon's firing of Special Watergate Prosecutor Archibald Cox and the subsequent resignation in rapid order of Attorney General Elliot Richardson and his deputy, William Ruckelshaus,—the widely publicized "Saturday night massacre" in late October, 1973—a week had rarely passed in which a senator or congressman or some prominent columnist or editor had not called upon Mr. Nixon to resign. For the next eight months, the House Judiciary Committee impeachment inquiry into Mr. Nixon's conduct following the Watergate burglary cover-up appeared mired in the White House strategy of obstruction and delay. The President's ability to dominate the news clearly overshadowed the private, executive sessions of the obscure, little-understood congressional committee investigating his alleged misconduct in office. Indeed, many long-time Washington observers continued to question whether the Constitution's abbreviated clauses on the impeachment power, vested in Congress, would be workable when applied to a President of the United States who had amassed the most one-sided electoral college mandate since George Washington. Would the American Constitution, written for a largely rural seaboard society two centuries ago, function effectively to check and impeach a chief executive who, using the vast powers of his office, had achieved worldwide diplomatic success in China and the Soviet Union, who had ended an eight-year American involvement in Indochina, and who, with Secretary of State Henry Kissinger, had recently succeeded in bringing the warring Arab countries and Israel to the Middle Eastern peace table? Would a 435-member House of Representatives, representing the varied interest groups of 50 states and often bogged down by its inability to agree on a sustained course of action, be able to face the President head-on and charge him with a 29-count list of impeachable offenses?

Though more than a dozen of his staff members had been convicted of Watergate-related offenses, President Nixon appeared to be weathering the storm until the U.S. Supreme Court, in late July, 1974, ruled against the President's claimed unlimited right to "executive privilege" (to retain White House taped conversations). The court's ruling was a clear restatement of the principle established by its decision in 1803 *(Marbury* v. *Madison),* that the Supreme Court was the final arbiter of the meaning of the Constitution. Faced with a Supreme Court order to turn over 147 taped conversations thought to contain highly incriminating evidence against him, Mr. Nixon's chances of surviving impeachment faded rapidly. The second body blow to President Nixon came within a week, when the House Judiciary Committee voted by a resounding bipartisan majority to recommend to the full House three articles of impeachment.

Mr. Nixon apparently saw the handwriting on the wall. Six days later, he admitted in a statement accompanying the release of transcripts of three taped White House conversations that he had ordered a halt to the FBI investigation of the covert financing operation of the Watergate burglars. This admission triggered a flood of proimpeachment demands on Capitol Hill, including a majority of the members of his own party. Mr. Nixon's staunchest defenders on the House Judiciary Committee reversed themselves, and all ten Republican members who had voted against all three impeachment articles came out against Mr. Nixon. Assistant Senate Republican Minority Leader Robert Griffin of Michigan and a group of his Republican colleagues demanded that Mr. Nixon resign or face a swift impeachment vote in the U.S. Senate. Three nights later, in a nationwide televised address, Mr. Nixon sorrowfully announced his resignation as President of the United States—the first chief executive in American history to resign from office.

In retrospect, the remarkably evenhanded and thorough performance of the Judiciary Committee's impeachment hearing—the first step in the process to remove a President—led to the almost universal judgment that the Constitution's impeachment clauses were working as the founding fathers had intended. Actions by the Supreme Court and the House Judiciary Committee showed that they were not persuaded by the view frequently expressed by President Nixon during the long Watergate investigation that he was acting to preserve the presidency from legislative encroachment for the benefit of all future chief executives. More importantly, these judicial and legislative decisions demonstrated more convincingly than any other action since the framers met in Philadelphia that the system of checks and balances and the separation of powers are the most effective way to prevent abuses of power. This theme will recur frequently throughout our study as we analyze the various roles performed by the President and Congress.

THE PRESIDENTIAL-CONGRESSIONAL SEE-SAW: HISTORICAL OVERVIEW

The constitutional system designed by the founding fathers is one in which conflict and cooperation between the President and Congress are a requirement for the system of government to work. A leading authority on the presidency, Edward S. Corwin, concluded that:

> In short, the Constitution reflects the struggle between two conceptions of executive power: that it ought always to be subordinate to the supreme legislative power, and that it ought to be, within generous limits, autonomous and self-directing; or in other terms, the idea that the people are *re-presented* in the Legislative *versus* the idea that they are *embodied* in the Executive. Nor has this struggle ever entirely ceased, although on the whole it is the latter theory that has prospered. . . . Taken by and large, the history of the presidency has been a history of aggrandizement . . . [1]

The Constitution allows and encourages each branch to be captured by different interests, so that in the words of James Madison, "Ambition must be made to counteract ambition."[2] This built-in conflict, Madison believed, would serve to protect individual rights providing that no branch could dominate the entire government.

Framers' Intentions

The writings of John Locke, brilliant seventeenth-century English philosopher, justifying the Glorious Revolution, provided strong support for the "separation of powers" doctrine.

Locke wrote in his famous *Two Treatises of Government* (1689) that under a free government the "legislative is not only the supreme power, [but is] sacred and unalterable in the hands where the community has once placed it." In a later chapter he states that "Where the legislative and executive power are in distinct hands, as they are in all . . . well-framed governments, there the good society requires that several things should be left to them that has the executive power." [3] He also set down a formula for dividing power between the executive and legislative branches to create a "balanced constitution." Locke's work was read and widely discussed by the authors of the Constitution—it was their Bible for democracy. The framers incorporated this principle of "separation of powers" by prescribing to the Congress in Article I of the Constitution the "legislative powers herein granted;" the President was granted the "executive power of the United States" in Article II, and the judicial power of Article III was to be exercised by the Supreme Court and all lower courts created by Congress.

There can be little doubt that the decisions of the founding fathers at the Constitutional Convention represented a victory for those who favored a strong and independent executive. However, this was certainly not a foregone conclusion when the delegates met in May of 1787. The Virginia Plan, prepared chiefly by James Madison, and the New Jersey Plan, presented by William Paterson, both called for selection of the executive by the legislative branch. No less than five times during the course of the convention the delegates rejected this method of selection. It was not until the closing days of the convention that Gouverneur Morris, Chairman of the Committee of Eleven, proposed the use of a separate electoral college for the selection of the President. The authors of the Constitution had come within a whisker of establishing an executive selected by the legislative branch.

In the final vote, the presidency was made a singular office which did not need the approval of a council to act. Furthermore, the presidency would have a constitutional basis separate from the legislative branch. The founding fathers accepted the view that legislatures were gathering all power unto themselves and needed to be checked by a strong and independent executive. Madison, in No. 48 of the *Federalist Papers,* complained that "the legislative department was everywhere expanding its sphere of activity, and drawing all power into its impetuous vortex." [4] Clearly, the intention of a majority of the framers was to swing the distribution of power in the national government back to a "balanced government." They provided checks to prevent dominance by one branch. Gouverneur Morris, in a speech before the convention, emphasized the need for checking the legislative power with a vigorous executive. He pointed out that the " . . . one great object of the Executive is to control the Legislature. The Legislature will continually seek to aggrandise and perpetuate themselves; and will seize those critical moments produced by war, invasion, or convulsion for that purpose." [5]

The "checks and balances," then, were designed to prevent too great an aggrandizement of power in the hands of any branch.[6] Congress would have the final say in determining the number and scope of activities of executive agencies and departments. The President would control high-level appointments in the agencies—but only after senate confirmation. The Congress could pass legislation and the President could veto the legislation. To override the President's veto, Congress would be required to muster a two-thirds majority in both houses. The President, as "commander-in-chief," could order troops into action, but Congress was given the power to decide whether to support this executive action by a declaration of war and by its "power of the purse."

Early Contests between Congress and President

George Washington's support of a strong national government, coupled with the widely held belief that he would become the first President aided the forces who favored a strong and independent presidency. His powerful role is attested to by the statement of Pierce Butler, a delegate from South Carolina, who wrote, "I do not believe they (the executive powers) would have been so great had not many members cast their eyes toward

General Washington as President; and shaped their ideals of the powers to be given the President, by their opinion of his virtue." [7]

As the first President, Washington established precedents for executive-legislative relations in order to fill in "gray areas" left unanswered by the Constitution. Nonetheless, three major conflicts developed during Washington's two terms in office. The first question concerned whether the President alone, under his duty to "take care that the laws be faithfully executed," or the Senate and President, as a logical extension of the "advise and consent" clause of appointing executive officials, or the Congress, under the "necessary and proper clause," should control the removal of principal executive officers. The House decided that the President alone had the power, and Vice-President John Adams cast a tie-breaking vote in the Senate to ensure the President this power. The language of the act creating the Department of Foreign Affairs and all other new departments supported the power of the President under the Constitution to remove principal executive officers without consulting Congress.[8] Walter Hickel, secretary of the interior in the first Nixon Administration, was dismissed for lack of support of the Cambodian invasion. Presidents have never failed to remove a high-level executive officer because of any supposed lack of jurisdiction.

A second contest involved Washington's Proclamation of Neutrality in April, 1793, upon the outbreak of the Napoleonic Wars. A presidential rather than congressional act, this move was justified by Hamilton in several articles originally published in the *Gazette of the United States* under the pseudonym of Pacificus. Hamilton argued that the opening lines of Article II, "Executive power shall be vested in a President of the United States," gave the President inherent powers. He cited the removal power, the power to recognize foreign governments, and the power to judge our treaty obligations as prerogatives of the President. To Hamilton the general wording of the Constitution granted wide discretion to the President, whereas the more restrictive powers of the Congress in Article I to have "all legislative powers herein granted" represented a narrower grant of power. James Madison, writing under the pseudonym of Helvidius, challenged

Taft

Calhoun

Webster

Clay

Hamilton's broad view of executive prerogative. He claimed this justification to "strike at the vitals of the Constitution" could not be found in the Constitution but must be found in "royal prerogative in the British government." [9] Again, the executive prevailed in the second major contest with Congress. The "Nixon Doctrine" on commitment of American forces only when our national security is at stake is the present-day extension of this vast power.

In the third controversy, Washington refused to provide requested documents to the Republican-controlled House of Representatives when Ambassador John Jay was negotiating the Treaty of Paris. Washington's response was that "a just regard to the Constitution and to the duty of my office . . . forbid a compliance with your request." [10] Thus, the principle of "executive privilege" was established. Nearly every President in American history has asserted his powers to withhold documents that would hinder the exercise of his executive functions. President Nixon applied this principle extensively during the early stages of the Watergate investigation. The legitimacy and limits of executive privilege were dealt with by the Supreme Court in July, 1974. (See Chapter 6.)

Although a number of confrontations occurred between the executive and legislative branches during Washington's Administrations, a significant degree of joint-party leadership developed during the first eight years of the Republic: The Judiciary Act of 1789, establishing the federal court system, was approved; measures that created the executive departments were largely a product of action by the House; and the "Great Reports" drafted by Hamilton exemplified the executive leadership of the legislature.[11]

Early Congressional Ascendancy

John Adams' presidency was marked by growing congressional assertion of control over government policy. Funds for an expanded army were appropriated and the controversial Alien and Sedition Acts were passed over presidential objections.

Hamilton controlled the votes of the President's own Federalist party in the Congress.

Thomas Jefferson, Adams' successor, was outwardly deferential to Congress. In his first message to that body he concluded "that nothing shall be wanting on my part to inform, as far as in my power, the legislative judgment, nor to carry that judgment into faithful execution."[12] Jefferson's success as a President, however, rested upon his party leadership and control of his party in the Congress. For example, Jefferson used the Chairman of the Ways and Means Committee, John Randolph, to manage his legislative program during his first term. Jefferson also used the congressional caucus and the patronage system to attain his legislative objectives. His own success with Congress emphasized the need for strong party leadership from the White House if the President were to accomplish his goals.

The tremendous power of the congressional caucus was evident when it selected Madison and Monroe to serve as President. Throughout their terms both Presidents were in fact held accountable to this body. Binkley concludes that "by 1808 the caucus had become powerful enough to pass from being an instrument for executive control of Congress and start on its career of the control of the Executive."[13] One reason for this control was that both Madison and Monroe lacked the skill needed to control the leadership of their own party in Congress. Whereas Jefferson had sought candidates to run against those who voted against administration programs,[14] these Presidents did not even attempt to have a voice in the selection of the Speaker of the House.[15] The names of Clay, Calhoun, and Webster dominated the leadership of the nation during this period. It is not surprising that Congress exercised more power during the first quarter of the nineteenth century, for it controlled the selection of the President, either through nomination by "King Caucus" or, as in 1800 and 1825, by election in the House of Representatives.

Jackson became President not through the choice of members of Congress but through the support of the citizenry. The "plebiscitary presidency" of Jackson coincided with the death of "King Caucus," the elimination of legislative selection of presidential

House Brawl

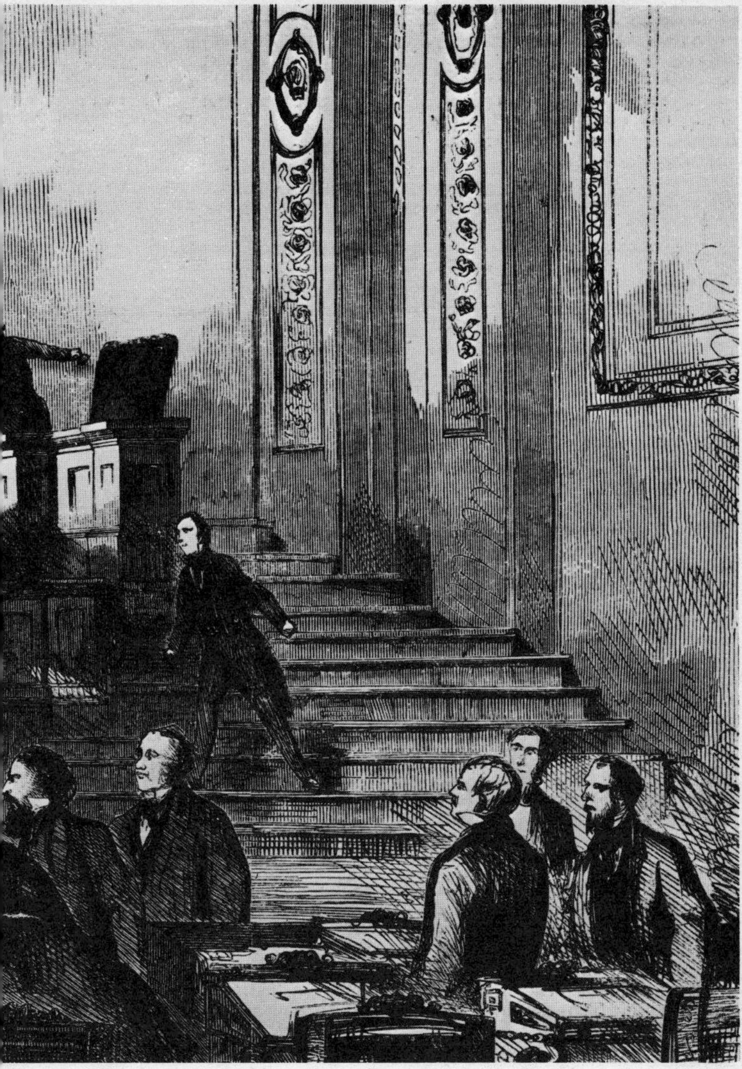

electors, and the start of their selection by the people. Jackson used the national convention to connect the presidential selection process directly to the people and not to Congress. He therefore claimed to represent the people as a whole.

In vetoing the rechartering of the Second Bank of the United States, Jackson confidently asserted that his authority came from the Constitution, and neither the Supreme Court nor Congress could interfere with his interpretation of the constitutionality of a law.[16] Throughout his two terms he made it clear that as a coequal branch of government he would make vigorous use of the veto power. However, his reliance on the veto power was a negative force on Congress and did not provide positive executive leadership of that body. The country would have to wait for the national emergency of the Civil War before turning to a strong President.

After Jackson, the Whig theory of executive subordination to Congress was dominant, except during the term of President Polk, in the years before the Civil War. William Henry Harrison, the first Whig President, summed up his view of the President's role in his inaugural address:

> I cannot conceive that by fair construction any or either of its (the Constitution's) provisions would be found to constitute the President a part of the legislative power. . . . And it is preposterous to suppose that could be entertained for a moment that the President, placed at the capital, in the center of the country could better understand the wants and wishes of the people than their immediate representatives who spend a part of every year among them . . . and (are) bound to them by the triple tie of interest, duty, and affection.[17]

Harrison's successor, John Tyler, was also a Whig by philosophy, but his vetoes of attempts to reestablish a Bank of the United States led to the first serious attempt to impeach a President. Tyler, however, was able to avoid this threatened impeachment.

President James Polk sought and received from Congress a reduced tariff, reestablishment of an independent treasury, boundary settlement of the Oregon territory dispute, and the acquisition of California after the Mexican War. Polk's presidency, however, was followed by a resurgence of the congressional Whigs, who dominated Presidents Taylor, Fillmore, Pierce, and Buchanan. As a result, Congress became the focal point for the great debates over slavery—until the election of President Abraham Lincoln in 1860.

Lincoln: Prototype of the Modern President

When Lincoln came to the presidency, many observers regarded him as too inexperienced to deal with the awesome task lying before him. His predecessor, James Buchanan, had vacillated over whether he did or did not have the authority to act in the face of the threats of various states to secede from the Union. The country did not have to wait long for Lincoln to act. Lincoln exercised more power than any President before him and perhaps more than any President following him in the office. Professor Binkley has commented that "unquestionably the high-water mark of the exercise of executive power in the United States is found in the administration of Abraham Lincoln." [18] The civil war President never doubted that he had the power necessary to halt the southern rebellion.

Lincoln concluded that as commander-in-chief and in conjunction with his "duty to take care that the laws be faithfully executed" he must act to preserve the Union at all costs. Without consulting Congress, he clamped a blockade on southern ports, enlarged the regular army by 22,000 and the navy by 18,000 men, and called for 42,000 volunteers for three years' service. The latter action was a clear disregard of the constitutional delegation to Congress "to raise and support armies." He advanced over $2 million to private citizens to purchase goods for the government; he pledged the credit of the United States for a large loan; he closed the mails to treasonable correspondence; and he suspended the writ of habeas corpus between Washington and New York to guarantee that the lines of communication would not be disrupted. Then he called Congress into special session, eleven weeks after the initial attack on Fort Sumter, and invited the lawmakers to support his actions retroactively. "These measures," he stated, "whether strictly legal or not, were ventured upon under what appeared to be a popular demand and a public necessity, trusting then, as now, that Congress would readily ratify them. It is believed that *nothing has been done beyond the constitutional competence of Congress.*" [19] Congress approved these acts "as if they had been issued and done under the previous express authority and direction of the Congress of the United States." [20]

Lincoln and the "whiggish" members of his party clashed over who possessed the authority to control the conduct of the war and the reconstruction policy to be followed after the conflict ended. On December 20, 1861, radical Republicans in the Congress appointed a Joint Committee on the Conduct of the War. They sent investigating missions to the front, which tended to undermine army discipline. One of their early accomplishments was the replacement of Secretary of War Cameron with a man of their own selection, Edwin M. Stanton. Who would carry on the war? Senator Charles Sumner, among others, supported the Whig doctrine of congressional supremacy by declaring, "I claim for Congress all that belongs to any government in the exercise of the right of war," and he concluded that "It is by an act of Congress that the war powers are set in motion. When once in motion the President must execute them. But he is only the *instrument of Congress* under the Constitution of the United States." [21] Lincoln, however, freely appointed military governors in territory occupied by the army and relieved commanding generals as he saw fit.

By executive order, Lincoln issued the famous Emancipation Proclamation on September 22, 1863, freeing all slaves in Confederate-held territory. This act was performed without consulting Congress—and after it had adjourned.

Lincoln issued another proclamation in December, 1863, which set down rules for Reconstruction and readmission of states into the Union under very liberal terms. Congress responded with the Wade-Davis Bill, which would have required

50 percent rather than 10 percent of the citizens to support the Union before the state would be readmitted. Lincoln pocket-vetoed this bill and made the election of 1864 a referendum on who should control Reconstruction. Lincoln won reelection easily. Lincoln's position on his clashes with Congress over which branch was to be dominant is summarized in a remark he made when he pocket-vetoed the Wade-Davis Bill: "I conceive that I may, in an emergency, do things on military grounds which cannot constitutionally be done by Congress."[22] Presidents since Lincoln have responded to "crises" and "emergencies" by using the inherent powers of the office, but none has exceeded the grand sweep which he applied to these powers.

Post-Civil War Congressional Dominance

Andrew Johnson came to the presidency destined to confront a Congress angered by the excesses of the Lincoln Administration and determined to reassert its dominance. Only a few hours after Lincoln died, a group of radical Republicans caucused and decided to rid the President's cabinet "of the last vestige of Lincolnism."[23] The temporarily enfeebled presidency received its greatest challenge on February 24, 1868, when the House of Representatives, by a margin of 126 to 47, voted eleven articles of impeachment against the President. Ten articles were aimed at the President's removal of Secretary of War Edwin M. Stanton, an act which violated the Tenure of Office Act, passed on March 2, 1867. The eleventh article was purely a political charge. Johnson had criticized Congress for its vengeful attitude toward the southern states in its reconstruction policies. The House charged that Andrew Johnson did, on August 8, 1866, "deliver with a loud voice certain intemperate, inflammatory, and scandalous harangues, and did therein utter loud threats and bitter menaces as well against Congress as the laws of the United States duly enacted thereby."[24] Radical Republican hostility to Johnson's policies led to his impeachment. On May 16, 1868, after a two-month trial, the Senate voted guilty, 35, not guilty, 19, on each of the eleven counts. Under the two-thirds rule the President had escaped conviction by one vote! Another serious challenge to the tenure of the occupant of the White House would not be made until the passage of the 22nd Amendment in 1951, which limited Presidents to two full terms. More than a century passed after the Johnson impeachment trial before another President, Richard Nixon, faced a major impeachment inquiry.

During the latter half of the nineteenth century congressional aggressiveness seemingly placed the presidency in permanent eclipse. Woodrow Wilson's classic *Congressional Government* (1885) describes the focus of power in the national government as follows:

> ... the actual of our present government is simply a scheme of congressional supremacy. ... It is said that there is no single or central force in our federal scheme ... but only a balance of powers and a nice adjustment of interactive checks, as all the books say. How is it, however, in the practical conduct of the federal government? In that, unquestionably, the predominant and controlling force, the center and source of all motive and of all regulative power, is Congress. ... Congress (is) the dominant, nay, the irresistible, power of the federal system ... that high office (the presidency) has fallen from its first estate of dignity because its power has waned; and its power has waned because the power of Congress has become predominant.[25]

These passages indicate that the presidency had become completely subordinate to Congress under Presidents such as Grant, Hayes, Arthur, and Benjamin Harrison. In the 1880's, the noted British political scientist, James Bryce, observed that "The expression of his (the President's) wishes conveyed to Congress in messages has not necessarily any more effect on Congress than an article in a prominent party newspaper." [26]

Three major reasons may be put forth to explain congressional dominance of the executive branch during this period. Congress, from the passage of the Tenure of Office Act, which preceded the Johnson impeachment trial, through the next 30 years, challenged the chief executive over appointment and control of personnel in the executive branch. Congress insisted upon the advice and consent of the Senate in the selection of high officials as well as subordinates. Controllers and auditors in the Treasury Department as well as coiners and even melters in local mints were subject to senate confirmation.[27] Congress also insisted on controlling the day-to-day operations of the executive departments and agencies.

A second major reason for congressional dominance during this period was its control of the purse and its careful specificity in legislation. Congress forbade the transfer of funds from one year to another. One observer of the period notes, "On the major legislation of the era—reconstruction, currency, tariffs, veterans' affairs, interstate commerce—Congress left a heavy imprint." [28] Congress intruded into day-to-day operations by attaching substantive legislation to appropriations bills which the President dared not veto. In addition, Congress enacted legislative details ordinarily delegated to administrators, such as renaming the steam yacht *Fanny* and repairing the fence around the cemetery at Harpers Ferry.[29] So assertive was Congress that Grover Cleveland used 414 vetoes in his first term to turn back the tide of legislative domination.

A third factor explaining congressional dominance during this era was the lack of emergencies and crises requiring presidential action. Depressions, urban and rural poverty, and the strikes and riots of the period were viewed as within the jurisdiction of state and local governments. Congress and the courts had excluded the national government from oversight of the industrial giants. The presidency was not viewed as operating at the center of national politics.

In his first message, President Chester Arthur asked Congress, for power to deal with bands of cowboys terrorizing the Southwest. Congress ignored his request. Unlike Polk and Lincoln before him, Arthur was unwilling to use his presidential prerogatives to achieve his objectives.[30] Except for the brief Spanish-American War, pursued mainly because congressional "war-hawks" demanded action, the Presidents of this period did not have many opportunities to exercise the sweeping powers that Presidents of the twentieth century have used to aggrandize their office.

As a matter of fact, attempts were made during the post-Civil War period to permanently cripple the presidency. Horace Greeley championed a constitutional amendment to restrict Presidents to one term in office. The Pendleton Committee proposed that cabinet members be authorized to sit in the House and Senate and be required to attend sessions twice a week for the purpose of supplying information. Had these proposals been successful, the Congress "would have upset the balance of power" in the federal government, and, as Leonard White concludes, "would have weakened the President's effective participation in departmental business by increasing the authority of Congress and its committees."[31]

The Presidency Comes of Age: TR to FDR

Two great forces account for the rise of the presidency and the establishment of a new congressional-presidential relationship in the twentieth century. One was the economic changes brought about by the advancement of industrial technology in the late nineteenth century, coupled with changing views of the responsibility of the federal government for controlling these new economic forces. The second major force altering congressional-presidential relationships and adding to the power of the presidency was the emergence of the United States as a world power.

Before 1890, the gospel of *laissez-faire* dominated the relationship between government and industry. Few statutes were passed to protect the public from the giant economic combinations which were increasingly dominating national life. After the passage of the Interstate Commerce Act in 1887, no fewer than 38 major laws were passed to give the national government regulatory power over industry.[32] Congress attempted to put much of this regulatory power in the hands of independent com-

"Yo, DICKS"

"Czar" Reed

Theodore Roosevelt

missions; yet much of this power ultimately resided in the executive branch.

Theodore Roosevelt is remembered as the first great reformer of the modern industrial era. He revealed in his autobiography that in the anthracite coal strike of 1902 he had planned to use army troops to run the mines if a settlement had not occurred. Taft, while less falmboyant than Roosevelt, was no less vigorous and proposed the 16th Amendment, which made a graduated income tax possible in 1913. This amendment opened a huge reservoir of funds for the federal government, which could be employed by future Presidents for social and economic programs for the downtrodden of the nation.

The inability of Congress, through its numerous appropriations and revenue committees, to coordinate a comprehensive budget led eventually to an executive-controlled budget. President Taft's Commission on Economy and Efficiency first suggested a national budgeting system in 1912. In 1919 a select committee of the House of Representatives proposed a national budget under presidential control, vested in a bureau of the Treasury Department. Finally, in 1921 the passage of the Budget and Accounting Act eliminated the freedom the departments had had to submit requests for money directly to Congress. Henceforth, budget requests would come from the President. The major impact of this centralization of budget making was to strengthen the President's hand in dealing with Congress and with the departments, agencies, and bureaus under his jurisdiction. The "Budget Message" has become a basis for presidential leadership of Congress and directing of the federal bureaucracy. The institutionalized presidency was coming of age.

The second major expansive force which added power to the presidency during this period was the United States' activity in foreign affairs. From 1900 to the outbreak of World War I Congress generally chose to watch quietly as United States military forces were used for numerous "expeditions" and "interventions" in such places as China, Haiti, Cuba, Mexico, Honduras, and Panama. Public opinion seemed to favor American military activity, and Congress did not choose to step into this area of executive prerogative. At the turn of the century, for example, President McKinley sent American troops to China during the Boxer Rebellion, without congressional approval. In one instance when Congress balked at an executive action, Commander-in-Chief Theodore Roosevelt sent the fleet halfway around the world and left it up to Congress to buy enough coal to bring the fleet back home. In 1916 President Wilson did not hesitate to send American troops deep into Mexico without Congressional approval.

World War I brought to the presidency the opportunity to use powers which had not been exercised since the Civil War—and to use other powers which had never been exercised. Wilson was delegated the authority to take over and operate the railroads, regulate and prohibit exports, commandeer factories, withhold fuel, and fix transportation priorities. Unlike Lincoln, Wilson sought and received from Congress expressed legislative authority for almost every unusual step he undertook. "The source of Lincoln's power was the Constitution, and he operated in spite of Congress," writes one presidential authority, "[while] the source of Wilson's power . . . was a batch of statutes, and he cooperated with Congress." [33] International events of the twentieth century and the enormous military potential of the United States, especially since World War II, have added greatly to the powers exercised by modern Presidents.

The personalities of Presidents and the views they brought to the office also had an impact upon congressional-presidential relations and added new dimensions to presidential authority. Theodore Roosevelt, for one, "gave the Presidency an organic connection with Congress," which goes far to explain his own legislative success.[34] He understood the responsibilities, affiliations, and needs of legislators and had an instinct for calculating the personal power of those on Capitol Hill. No sooner had Joseph Cannon been elected Speaker of the House of Representatives, then Roosevelt invited him to the White House. He became a frequent visitor and conveyor of the President's wishes in legislation. Through "Czar" Cannon, Roosevelt attempted to systematize his function as "chief legislator." Cannon controlled the all-important Rules Committee and committee assignments in the House, and at that time even the Senate could repeatedly be bent to the will of "Uncle Joe." Characterizing the vision of Roosevelt and his own practicality in determining how programs could be funded, Cannon described their relationship years later:

> We did not always agree; in fact, we often disagreed but seldom on principle and usually as to practical methods. Roosevelt had the outlook of the Executive and the ambition to do things. I had the more confined outlook of the legislator who had to consider ways of meeting the expenditures of new departments and expansions in government.[35]

Roosevelt would gauge the needs of legislators and by trading prestige and favors achieve program results. It should not go without notice that the prestige of the House has never been as high as it was under the strong, centralized leadership of Cannon in the days before the congressional "revolt" of 1910.

Theodore Roosevelt believed in the personalization of the presidency to the point of writing his messages to Congress, addressed more to the larger national audience than to the legislators. He believed in his role as a molder and interpreter of public opinion. He put the presidency on the front pages of the nation's newspapers, where it has remained ever since, for he saw the office as a "bully pulpit" to be used for his purposes. Concerned that the Elkins Act, which would have forbidden railroad rebates, would be defeated by the "big interests" in the Senate, he leaked a story to the press that six senators had received telegrams from John D. Rockefeller on how to vote. The bill passed quickly after a public outcry.

Woodrow Wilson firmly believed that the President's duty "to give the Congress information of the State of the Union, and recommend to their Consideration such Measures as he shall judge necessary and expedient," [36] could be used as a source of power. Wilson delivered his State of the Union address in person, rather than merely dispatching it to Congress in written form.

This dramatized his position and gave him another avenue to the legislators, the press, and ultimately the people. As Wilson saw it, the presidency is the "intelligible government" with which the people can identify. Wilson often went to Congress to personally deliver special messages. After his address on the tariff bill, he lobbied with senators in the Senate President's Room and returned often to discuss legislative strategy with them.[37] Wilson believed in presidential involvement in all phases of the legislative process, and he made extensive use of party caucuses in each house to exert his will over Congress.

For a 12-year interim, Presidents Harding, Coolidge, and Hoover served in the White House with a general pledge not to be executive autocrats in their dealings with Congress. Herbert Hoover summed up his own belief and those of his two immediate predecessors about the misfortune of aggressive executive leadership by declaring that "The militant safeguard to liberty . . . [is] . . . legislative independence . . . the weakening of the legislative arm leads to encroachment by the executive upon individual liberty."[38] Faced with economic collapse during the Hoover Administration, the nation demanded a President who would not be timid in leading Congress and the nation out of the depths of the depression.

The New Deal Era: The White House Takes Over

When Franklin Delano Roosevelt won election in 1932, the nation was in such desperate straits that the day after the President's inauguration Will Rogers, the humorist, observed that "The whole country is with him just so he does something. If he burned down the Capitol, we would cheer and say 'Well, we at least got a fire started.'"[39] The massiveness of the economic collapse of the 1930's can hardly be exaggerated. Between 12 and 15 million men were unemployed; 45 percent of the blue-collar workers were out on the streets competing for jobs that did not exist; one family out of seven was receiving public relief; 4600 banks had closed their doors; auto plants in Michigan and textile factories in the South were closed; farmers let crops rot in the fields because it cost more to harvest them than they could sell them for at market. The economic chaos of the Great Depression and the mood of the nation demanded action and vigorous leadership—both were not long in coming under Roosevelt's Administration.

On March 4, 1933, Roosevelt laid the challenge facing the nation before the Congress in his inaugural address:

> It is to be hoped that the normal balance of executive and legislative authority may be wholly adequate to meet the unprecedented task before us. . . . I am prepared under my constitutional duty to recommend the measures that a stricken nation in the midst of a stricken world may require. . . . But in the event that the Congress shall fail to take these courses and in the event that the national emergency is still critical I shall not evade the clear course of duty that will then confront me. I shall ask the Congress for the one remaining instrument to meet the crisis—broad executive power to wage a war against the emergency as great as the power that would be given to me if we were invaded by a foreign foe.[40]

The President moved with breathtaking swiftness to deal with the crisis by calling for a special session of Congress to convene five days after his inaugural address. Then followed the famous "Hundred Days" during which more legislation was passed by Congress than at any other time in the history of the Republic. This went beyond any normal "honeymoon" between a newly elected President and Congress. The political climate in the nation and in Congress aided the display of movement, experimentation, and change. Relief, recovery, and reform were the goals and quick, decisive action was the method used to achieve them.

Both houses of Congress were under Democratic control, with 150 newly elected and inexperienced Democratic congressmen on hand. There was no semblance of the congressional leadership that had been provided by Speakers Reed and Cannon. The void was filled by Roosevelt, who with his immense energy proved to be an unprecedented mover and agitator in the widest range of legislative activity. His degree of support in Congress can be seen in the passage of the Emergency Banking Act. The bill had not been printed when the sole copy sent from the White House was read by the Clerk of the House. It was passed by both houses with little debate and promulgated by the President that evening. The Republican floor leader supported the banking bill with the explanation, "The House is burning down and the President of the United States says this is the way to put out the fire," and that was good enough for him.[41] Of the eleven major Roosevelt measures passed by Congress, one analysis indicates that there was an average of only three- and two-thirds days of debate on each measure.[42]

How did FDR fare with Congress once the air of crisis in government had ended? Even with the surprising gains for the Democrats in the off-year election of 1934, which seemed to endorse Roosevelt's actions, the President's "honeymoon" period was soon over, and it was back to presidential-congressional politics as usual—with a few Roosevelt alterations. Throughout the 1930's Roosevelt refined techniques which had been employed less effectively by his predecessors. The first was the presidential message. His cousin TR had indicated to a critic the unwisdom of proposing details of a bill when a message was sent to Congress. Wilson had used the presidential message to focus attention on his measures. Franklin Roosevelt not only sent messages to Congress but also sent along carefully prepared bills (NRA, AAA, Lend-Lease) to accomplish the purpose of the message. From 1933 to 1938 he sent over 120 special messages to the Congress.

A second device employed by FDR to control legislation was the veto. At the close of his second term in 1941, FDR had vetoed 505 measures—over 30 percent of all measures disapproved by Presidents since 1792. That the veto is an effective device in the legislative process can be seen by the fact that from 1792 to 1941 only 49 of 1645 vetoes were overridden by the Congress.[43]

A third device of which Roosevelt made extensive use was patronage. Not since Woodrow Wilson, 12 years before, had a Democrat occupied the White House. In addition to the federal marshals, judges, postmasters, and high-level cabinet posts that were normally available, President Roosevelt was also able to appoint thousands to new offices in the relief and recovery agencies—all outside the merit system.

The most outstanding reason for FDR's early success with Congress and his later legislative achievements was the unprecedented support given to him by the American people. He would scan both critical and friendly newspapers each morning to take the pulse of people in Chicago, Philadelphia, Boston, and Saint Louis. In dealing with the press corps he would trade wisecracks with them, call them by their first names, and meet with them twice a week, year after year, to give them stories for their papers. FDR abolished the written question format and let the reporters interrogate him orally. By such activity he dominated the front page in a way that no President before or since has. He was the first President to master the techniques of communication with the people directly over the radio. One observer notes that "In his fireside chats, he talked like a father discussing public affairs with his family in the living room." [44] He had occasional setbacks, such as when he tried to pack the Supreme Court in 1937; yet he knew how to rally the people behind his legislative programs.

Congressional Eclipse in the Modern Era

Since World War II the presidency has generally overshadowed the Congress as an elephant towers over a mouse. The growth of presidential domination over Congress is paralleled by two major changes in the scope and responsibilities of the national government in the last quarter century: the development of "big government," especially since the New Deal, and the increasing involvement of the United States in the world arena —especially as protector of the "free world" following World War II.

The expansion of the activities of the national government is best illustrated by examining the phenomenal rate of growth of federal budget expenditures since the 1930's. The average expenditure level for the national government was slightly over $5 billion during the first half of the 1930's; it doubled to over $10 billion during the last half of the decade. Following the wartime expansion of the early 1940's, the budget leveled off, averaging over $40 billion during the late 1940's. The budget expenditures surpassed $100 billion for the first time in fiscal year 1966, exceeded $200 billion in fiscal year 1972, and topped $300 billion in fiscal year 1975.[45] The budget has increasingly reflected presidential priorities since the executive-budgeting system was established in 1921 and placed in the Executive Office of the President in 1939.

Corresponding to the growth of the budget has been the size of the federal bureaucracy. The portion of the bureaucracy most directly under the president's control and supervision is the Executive Office of the President (EOP). This office of the presidency was created in 1939 and included the White House Office and the Bureau of the Budget, which was transferred from the Treasury Department to the EOP. In 1946 the Council of Economic Advisors and in 1947 the National Security Council were created and attached to the EOP. The acts creating these agencies added greater presidential control over economic and national security affairs. Ten offices and councils were created during the 1960's and 1970's and attached to the Executive Office of the President.[46] These agencies cost $100 million to operate in 1973, a figure which exceeds annual expenditures for the entire federal government during much of the nineteenth century.[47] President Nixon had noted the expansion of the EOP from 570 employees in 1939 to 4216 staff members in 1973.[48] This is a far cry from the lone presidential assistant who advised Woodrow Wilson or the two presidential aides assigned to assist Herbert Hoover.

It was noted earlier in the chapter in discussing the creation of the Bureau of the Budget in 1921 that the presidency had begun to become institutionalized. It had become less a personal exercise of power by the President and more a division of labor among subordinates. The growth of government following the Great Depression and World War II has led to the coming of age of the "institutionalized presidency." This presidential establishment can operate in many ways without the active participation of the President. Activities which were formerly considered the President's work are now performed by advisors, aides, and special counsels who have proliferated extensively during the modern era. The Council on Economic Policy, Domestic Council, Office of Consumer Affairs, Council on Environmental Quality, and so forth now make decisions formerly reserved for presidential action alone. The "swelling of the presidency" has meant that many who perform tasks in the White House do not work directly with the President to carry out their functions. A story of what occurred in the White House in 1956 at the time of President Eisenhower's heart attack illustrates how the nature of the presidency changes when it is institutionalized. It was reported that many of those working in the White House did not know of the President's illness until they read it in the newspaper. A joke which made the rounds of Washington went like this:

Presidential Aide A — What if Ike died and Nixon became President?
Presidential Aide B — That would be rough, but what if Sherman Adams died and Ike became President?

This hypothetical exchange illustrates the crucial decision-making role of the staff of the President. Sherman Adams was the President's "chief of staff," and it is reported that he cleared nearly all important memos and documents before Eisenhower entered into the decision-making process.

The scope of the national government's activities has increased a hundredfold into areas not even dealt with by the federal government during the early 1930's. The national government administers a space program, subsidizes rents for low-income families, finances housing projects, and oversees the use of atomic energy among its hundreds of new activities. This sudden expansion has increased the responsibilities and supervision of the President in the postwar era. The relationship between Congress and the President in contemporary domestic affairs is examined in Chapter 6.

The second major factor leading to increased presidential power is the expanding commitments of the United States throughout the world. Since World War II the United States has become an active member in the United Nations, fought two major (undeclared) wars, sent troops to a dozen countries, and pledged this nation in treaties to defend 43 separate nations. The President has exercised his leadership in foreign affairs and military policy, and Congress has only recently attempted to reestablish a balance of power with the executive. In the following chapter the question of who can provide leadership for the nation is examined. Chapters 4 and 5 explore the relationship between the executive and legislative branches in foreign and military affairs.

Conclusion

As this review of the presidential-congressional see-saw has indicated, a crucial factor in the relationship between the two branches has been the nature of the times and the role of leadership assumed by the occupant of the White House and those who exercise power on Capitol Hill. Abraham Lincoln was a strong leader during the Civil War; Woodrow Wilson exercised aggressive leadership during the First World War; Franklin D. Roosevelt was forceful in dealing with the economic collapse of the 1930's and Second World War because the nation required swift and decisive action to deal with these national emergencies. The importance of focusing power during the cold war era led to support of presidential action when the national survival might have been threatened by military action abroad. Likewise, the nation has sought to curtail the use of executive power during periods of relative domestic and international calm. Following the Civil War, congressional leadership demanded and acquired ascendancy over domestic policy and a role in foreign affairs. The period following World War I witnessed reassertion of congressional power and direction of national affairs by Congress.

In addition to the role of the political climate of the times in determining which branch will exercise major control of national affairs, the role of leadership in the executive and legislative branches has been a major factor in determining which branch shall be predominate at any given time. From the time of Jefferson, strong Presidents have taken advantage of their access to party leadership to increase their control. Theodore Roosevelt and Woodrow Wilson worked closely with their party leadership in Congress to push through their legislative programs. A second device employed successfully by strong Presidents such as Theodore Roosevelt, Woodrow Wilson, Franklin Roosevelt, and the post-World War II Presidents has been the use of the mass media. By focusing national attention on their State of the Union addresses, fireside chats, press conferences, radio and television speeches, international summitry, and domestic and foreign travels they have been able to marshal public opinion and support behind their programs. Another device successful Presidents have used is the art of persuasion—performing favors for those who support them, such as patronage, "pork barrel" legislation, and White House invitations (presidential persuasion as a leadership resource is discussed further in Chapter 6). The other edge of the sword of presidential persuasion is the ability and willingness to punish those who oppose their programs—withholding favors, such as vetoing pet projects of their congressional adversaries.

Congressional leadership has occurred most often when Congress has been willing to turn over its vast powers to its strong internal leaders. This was the case under the leadership of Henry Clay, Daniel Webster, and John Calhoun in the pre-Civil War era, and Speakers of the House Thomas "Czar" Reed and Joseph G. Cannon in the closing decades of the nineteenth century. The leadership exercised by Lyndon Johnson as Senate Majority Leader and Sam Rayburn as Speaker of the House of Representatives in the 1950's was sufficient to provide a direction for the 535 members of Congress, who were willing to trade votes for political favors. Modern leadership in Congress has occurred more because of the political skills of the leaders than because of the structural power of their offices.

PRESIDENTIAL VERSUS CONGRESSIONAL LEADERSHIP

Since the days of George Washington, a controversy has persisted between the President and Congress over the locus of power in the American national government. Dramatized by the heated cabinet disputes between Alexander Hamilton and Thomas Jefferson in Washington's first administration, the debate over presidential versus congressional power is still very much alive in the 1970's. Clearly, part of the disagreement stems from the ambiguous language of Article II of the Constitution, which deals with executive power. As Henry Steele Commager has noted, "The Presidency has always given us trouble. It was, from the beginning, the 'dark continent' of American constitutionalism—the phrase is Charles A. Beard's." [1] Scholars have done little to clarify the question; for example, one writer notes, "The President represents the nation as a whole, while the Congress represents it as a collection of states and congressional districts." [2] More accurately, this controversy can be described as a dispute between those who favor executive leadership and those who favor legislative power—the "presidentialists" and the "congressionalists."

Presidentialists versus Congressionalists

The presidentialists favor giving the preeminent role of representing the national interest to the President. Proponents of this view have found widespread support among twentieth-century scholars. Conversely, the role of Congress has been consistently downgraded by these same writers. Professor Grant McConnell, for example, has commented on the weak performance of Congress in contrast to that of the President:

In the degree to which they prefer *national* interests, however, there is a significant distinction. The men of the Hill represent different publics, different from each other's and from the President's. Their constituencies are vastly different, some consisting largely of farmers, some of large cities, some of working-class districts, some of states where mining is overwhelmingly important, and so on; but the President's constituency consists of all of the people. Because the smaller constituencies emphasize particular interests the aggregate representation offered by Congress does not equal that of the presidency. The consequence is that there is consistently some difference between the policy positions of Congress and the President. On the whole, the President tends to emphasize national considerations and the interests of a great diversity of people more often than Congress.[3]

According to the late Clinton Rossiter, it is our complicated electoral process that "far too often places men with narrow views and special interests in the seats of power in Congress, yet acts remorselessly to reserve the Presidency for men with broad views and general interests, and thus with a deeper insight into the needs of the community." Rossiter also invites attention to "The sharp contrast between the traditions of the Presidency which call for strength and action, and the rules and customs of Congress, which place a high premium on caution and compromise."[4]

President Nixon reiterated the presidentialist view in a January, 1973, national press conference. In response to a question about his impoundment of appropriated funds, Mr. Nixon described the congressionalist view as follows:

> The difficulty, of course, and I have been a member of Congress, is that the Congress represents special interests. The Interior Committee wants more parks and the Agriculture Committee wants cheap R.E.A. loans and the HEW Committee or the Education and Labor Committee wants more for educa-

tion and the rest, and each of these wants we all sympathize with, but there is only one place in this Government where somebody has got to speak not for the special interests which the Congress represents but for the general interests.[5]

That one person, in Mr. Nixon's view, is of course the President.

The congressionalists, on the other hand, champion Congress as *the* more powerful branch. The constitutional primacy of the legislative branch has been well stated by Keefe and Ogul:

Despite the principle of separation of powers and the network of checks and balances, the mission of government rests basically upon the broad decisions of Congress. In the catalogue of government functions it is Congress which determines the broad policies and creates the administrative organizations to execute them, which fashions standards for administrative action and for the appointment and removal of administrative officials, which appropriates funds for the support of governmental functions, and which, in varying degrees, supervises and reviews the work of administrative establishments.[6]

Congressionalists never tire of pointing out that the Constitution makes certain that broad decisions regarding the major functions of government are entrusted to the legislative branch. Another staunch defender of the lawmakers, Ralph K. Huitt, reminds us that

Congress resembles the social system it serves; it reflects the diversity of the country. There is much to be said for a system in which almost every interest can find some spokesman, in which every cause can strike a blow, however feeble, in its own behalf.[7]

Congressionalists insist that the original constitutional formula of blended and coordinate powers is preferable to a strong presidential model in which Congress is relegated to a subordinate role of assenting to or confirming actions undertaken by the chief executive. Congress, these spokesmen believe, should serve as a countervailing power to that of the President and the federal bureaucracy.

Let's take a few moments to contrast the two main theories of leadership concerning the President and Congress.

Theories of Leadership

The *executive dominance* theory is reflected in President Nixon's view of executive leadership as quoted in the previous section. Other Presidents before him have voiced similar views. Woodrow Wilson, even before he reached the White House, declared that the President "is the only national voice in affairs." In contrast, Wilson noted, "There is no one in Congress to speak for the nation. Congress is a conglomeration of unharmonious elements. A collection of men representing each his neighborhood, each his local interest." [8] Speaking of the President's role as leader Wilson asserted, "He is the representative of no constituency, but of the whole people." President Truman echoed Wilson's view some 30 years later when he termed the President "the only lobbyist that all the 160 million people in this country have." [9]

Especially since the Roosevelt New Deal, many intellectuals have justified the executive dominance theory on the basis of one or both of the following two arguments: (1) that the majority which elects the President is more representative, and therefore more legitimate, than the congressional majorities; and (2) that the United States has entered a new era of continuing domestic and international crises, in which only the President, as the national leader, can respond with the required energy and speed to solve the problems facing the country. Ironically, it was at the very height of presidential power and prestige—at the outset of heavy American involvement in the Vietnam War—that this inflated view of the presidency first came under serious challenge. It also occurred at a time in history when congressional power and influence were at rock bottom. Before this revisionist attack on the presidency, one congressional critic declared, "Legislation has become much too complex politically to be effectively handled by a representative assembly. The primary work of legislation must be done, and increasingly is being done, by the three 'houses' of the executive branch: the bureaucracy, the administration, and the President." [10] In giving high marks to the White House, this same "high-flying" presidentialist supporter proclaimed, "The President now determines the legislative agenda of Congress almost as thoroughly as the British Cabinet sets the legislative agenda of Parliament." [11]

Defenders of the *legislative supremacy theory,* on the other hand, insist that Congress is "the center of a ring of institutions that compose the republic." [12] Advocates of the legislative supremacy theory point out that the founding fathers lavished their greatest attention on Congress, devoting some 1800 words of Article I of the U.S. Constitution to the powers of Congress. Moreover, the words in Article I are highly specific about the powers of Congress, whereas Article II on the presidency consists of fewer than 700 words, most of which concern the method of choosing the President and the qualifications prerequisite to being selected.

Many lawmakers insist that because Congress is closest to the people and more clearly reflects the judgment of the people, it holds the position of primacy within the American system of government. Proponents of the legislative supremacy theory argue that the President, in trying to represent all the voters, simply cannot give individual citizens the special attention and help that senators and representatives can. Advocates of the legislative supremacy theory concede, however, that until recently Congress has permitted its prerogatives to be dangerously eroded by the President. The ability to say "No," as James Burnham wrote almost two decades ago, is one of the central functions of a viable legislative branch. Supporters of the legislative supremacy theory believe that congressional oversight of the executive branch should be expanded through increased use of the General Accounting Office, stricter budgetary controls, regular investigative committee work, expanded congressional committee staffs, and detailed committee review of legislation, appointments, and appropriations.

Which of these two diametrically opposed theories of representation more closely approximates an accurate conception of what the founding fathers intended the power relationships between the President and Congress to be? No definite answer can be given to this question which has remained unsolved since the Constitutional Convention of 1787. This should cause no surprise because, as Wilfred Binkley noted years ago, defining the relationship between the executive and legislature was the "chief structural problem of the Constitutional Convention." [13]

Dual System of Representation

What actually evolved from the framers' deliberations is a system of dual representation—congressional and presidential. This was not exactly the original plan, since Madison and the other founders expected the popular majority to be represented and counted within the constituencies of Congress. The authors of the Constitution expected that the President would normally be elected by the House of Representatives, since the electoral college was not expected to provide a clear majority for any contender. In the first quarter of the nineteenth century, presidential candidates were in fact nominated by the Congressional caucus. But with the death of "King Caucus" in 1824 and the emergence of the Jacksonian party system, presidential candidates began to be nominated by the national party convention and elected by the whole male citizenry of the nation; consequently a second popular majority was "engrafted" on our political system.[14] Most party historians are convinced that the emergence of the national nominating convention and the Jacksonian view that the President was the party leader and popular spokesman eliminated forever the idea of presidential vassalage and absolute congressional domination of the President. No matter how many powerful congressional leaders challenged the President, they could never make him fully subservient to their wishes. Even beleaguered Presidents such as Tyler and Hayes were able to use the veto as a powerful defensive weapon.

This dual system of decision making that developed in America has generated both permanent conflict and the continuing necessity for cooperation between Congress and the President. But the dualism of the American political system ensures "that both the President and Congress will have powerful stakes in decision-making at the national level." [15] The founding fathers, anxious to avoid the abuses of untrammeled power, decided that each branch should exercise a degree of direct control over the other branches by authorizing each to play a part—although a limited part—in the exercise of the other's functions. As Richard C. Moe has commented:

> Madison was also convinced that a system that institutionalized conflict possessed a virtue beyond the simple checking of tyranny, for it contained the germ of a positive, energetic, competent government. Rather than becoming a source of division and stalemate, conflict within constitutional limits was perceived as a stimulus to the system's creative impulses.[16]

Over the years the two branches of government have formed "a kind of moving power equilibrium adapting to the increasing demands for central political decision, both essential to the equilibrium and neither able to innovate its power structure or decision-making precedures without affecting the other." [17] As noted by Thomas E. Cronin:

> Sometimes the presidency and sometimes Congress play the dominating role in initiating legislation. But the initiation as well as the enactment of virtually all major legislation in domestic and economic policy matters results from extensive 'conversations' between presidency and Congress, and between both of these institutions and strategic interest groups.[18]

Under these circumstances it seems naive to conceive of the presidency as representing the *national interest* or *general wel-*

fare and Congress as merely the tool of *special* or *particularistic interest.*[19] Furthermore, few major policies advocated by the President can ever be implemented without specific authorization from Congress. In normal times, neither the Congress nor the President has been able to dictate decisions to the other branch for any length of time. Indeed, throughout our history, the self-correcting dynamics of the American constitutional system have worked against unified control. As one commentator has observed, "The co-existence of an energetic executive with an equally energetic legislature is the foundation of political freedom in a pluralistic and continental society." [20]

This country has had several kinds of Presidents; a quick look at their success and failure provides an evaluation of the merits of each.

White House Leadership Models

A review of history shows that the Presidents fall into three classifications. The first category is termed the weak executive and is sometimes called the Whig or Buchanan type, which would also include James Madison and William Howard Taft. These Presidents all adhered to the strict construction of the Constitution. Indeed, President Buchanan viewed his office merely as the executor or administrator of acts of Congress. "My duty," he said, "is to execute the laws . . . and not my individual opinions." [21] He shrank from initiating any positive action, even in the face of threatened southern secession, and did nothing to prod Congress into national preparedness. In fact, he believed that he lacked the legal power to use force against the rebelling southerners.

The Whig view of the presidency includes subordination to the Congress and cautious use of those inherent prerogatives of the commander-in-chief and the executive powers. As one scholar observed, "In the Buchanan concept, the President has no undefined or residual powers of protecting the public welfare or dealing with national emergencies; he is limited to the powers expressly given him in the Constitution.[22]

The result of this concept of a weak executive finding shelter in the status quo was little social change or political innovation and a President with little influence on Capitol Hill. The Buchanan type of President rejects the idea that the Presidency is a political office; instead it is viewed as the administrative arm of Congress. President Taft spelled out the operative belief of the Whig President:

> The true view of the Executive function is . . . that the President can exercise no power which cannot be fairly and reasonably traced to some specific grant of power as proper and necessary to its exercise. Such specific grant must be either in the Federal Constitution or in an act of Congress passed in pursuance thereof. There is no undefined residium of power which he can exercise because it seems to him to be in the public interest.[23]

The second category of Presidents is the strong, bold executive, such as Lincoln, Jackson, Wilson, the two Roosevelts, Truman, Kennedy, Johnson, and Nixon. Frequently identified as the "Lincoln type," most of the strong Presidents have served in times of crisis—a war or a depression—and so have had the opportunity for the exceptional leadership that marked their administrations. Some have also served during periods of reform, such as the era of the progressive movement and the New Deal. This, too, accentuated their confident leadership. All were liberal in construing the Constitution; none hesitated to fill in the gaps with his own interpretation when the occasion arose. Accordingly, these strong executives are labelled presidentialists.

Theodore Roosevelt viewed the President as the "steward of the people." He believed that a President was obliged to act when circumstances demanded it, even if he could not find "some specific authorization to do it." As the "Rough Rider" President explained:

> My belief was that it was not only his right but his duty to do anything that the needs of the Nation demanded unless such

action was forbidden by the Constitution or by the laws. Under this interpretation of executive power, I did and caused to be done many things not previously done by the President and the heads of departments. I did not usurp power, but I did greatly broaden the use of executive power.[24]

Confident of their leadership ability, the strong executives are precedent-setters—sometimes stretching their powers to such an extent that the legality of their acts is questioned and even challenged in the courts. After the fall of France to Hitler in 1940, for example, President Franklin D. Roosevelt decided that to assure Great Britain's survival, he would turn over 50 older but well-equipped destroyers for 99-year leases on several British naval bases in the Caribbean. The destroyers were vitally necessary for British convoy duty in the North Atlantic against Nazi submarines; the leased bases helped our defenses in the western hemisphere—but were not crucial for our national survival. To make the trade, Roosevelt felt that he needed no more authorization than an "executive agreement" with Prime Minister Churchill. Some isolationist congressmen argued vehemently that the transfer of United States property to a foreign power and the acquisition of new military bases should require the consent of Congress. The only gesture Roosevelt made to placate Congress was to have his Attorney General, Robert Jackson, issue a legal opinion justifying the transaction, *after the fact*.

Six months before Pearl Harbor, FDR did not hesitate to seize the strikebound North American Aviation plant—without any specific legal authority. To justify his move, Roosevelt cited his own proclamation of an "unlimited emergency" as the main reason for the takeover of the plant that was producing fighter-bombers. Once again Attorney General Jackson found authority for the seizure in the "duty constitutionally and inherently resting upon the President to exert his civil and military as well as his moral authority to keep the defense efforts of the United States a going concern [and] to obtain supplies for which Congress has appropriated money, and which it has directed to the President to obtain."[25]

The strong President must inspire confidence even in times of adversity, as FDR did during the banking crisis of the Great Depression. His warm voice in all its resonant fullness came over the radio to say, "We have nothing to fear but fear itself," and a nation on the verge of panic moved forward in steadfastness and trust.

A strong President must use public techniques, such as all modes of communication, to formulate public opinion. Every message to Congress, every speech made around the country, and even his veto messages must be gauged to influence people. It has been all but forgotten now, but before the Watergate affair, President Nixon waged an effective battle of the budget against excessive congressional spending by a series of vetoes. Within a ten-day period in late March and early April, 1973, for example, Congress sustained Mr. Nixon on his vetoes of a $2.6 billion vocational rehabilitation bill and a $120 million water and sewer grant bill. In one veto message Mr. Nixon asserted that approval of the new measure would "represent a dangerous crack in the fiscal dam that this Administration has constructed to hold back a further flood of inflation or higher taxes or both." [26] In attempting to override the rural sewers veto, the House fell 51 votes short of the two-thirds vote needed for passage—a stunning victory for Mr. Nixon. By early November, 1973, President Nixon had vetoed 37 bills passed by Congress since his arrival in the White House, most on the grounds that either they stoked the inflationary fires or were "fiscally irresponsible." Other strong Presidents have used the veto weapon with even greater frequency. Presidents Franklin D. Roosevelt (633) and Harry S. Truman (250) accounted for more than a third of all presidential vetoes since 1789. The veto power is discussed at greater length in Chapter 6.

Theodore Roosevelt, the first modern President to recognize the power of the media, called the presidency a "bully pulpit," and delighted in taking his message "over the heads of Congress" directly to the people, whom he said are "the masters of both the Congress and the President." [27] But the most spectacular use of the direct approach came in the next generation. Franklin D. Roosevelt's famous "fireside chats" won the approval of the people for his New Deal program over a sometimes recalcitrant Congress.

The third category of Presidents is the paternal figure, illustrated first by Washington and more recently by Eisenhower. This type of executive seeks to be above party politics in an endeavor to govern for the good of all, somewhat like the philosopher-king described by Plato. However, Eisenhower borrowed something from both the Buchanan type and the Lincoln type. Although he conceived of his position as chiefly administrative, he vetoed bills which he considered ill-advised or catering to special interests. At a time when farmers were crying for price protection, Eisenhower vetoed a farm bill highly favorable to them, passed by the Democratic Congress to embarrass him. It was a costly bill and Congress knew it, but thought the President would be damaged either way, whether he signed or vetoed it. To the disappointment of the opposition, he vetoed it and then made a TV speech in which he explained why he did so and asked the Congress to send him a bill he could accept. Congress eventually passed a compromise measure that Mr. Eisenhower approved.

Following Washington's example, the paternal-figure President endeavors to rise above political divisions to build a national consensus. Author Sidney Hyman has summed up the Eisenhower conception of the chief magistrate and his duties:

> All men are by nature good, Government alone corrupts them. Therefore, to the extent that governments can be reduced in importance, the natural goodness of men will assert itself in social cooperation, voluntarily given. However irreconcilable rival interests may seem to be, once their representative men sit down and talk things over without the intervention of government, natural goodness will resolve all difficulties. His own Presidential function, then, was to be 'the President of all the people.'[28]

This approach includes the concept of a President as chief broker and consensus builder. While the retired Allied Supreme

Commander in World War II may have wished that partisan conflict could be transcended and that people could reason in an atmosphere of goodwill, the political process—especially at the national level—seldom operates in this fashion.

This leads to our next question: How does a President exert leadership?

The President as Persuader

As indicated earlier, the President can exercise broad authority in foreign affairs, but in domestic matters his real power does not depend so much upon his formal authority as upon his persuasive ability. Former White House staffer Richard Neustadt recalls President Truman's keen appreciation of this fact: "I sit here all day trying to persuade people to do things they ought to have sense enough to do without my persuading them . . . that's all the powers of a president amount to." [29] Mr. Truman was deliberately discounting his power somewhat, but he thoroughly understood from bitter experience that in the absence of responsible political parties the machinery of checks and balances restrains and hampers the President at every turn. Because the President is not an absolute ruler, but must share his powers with Congress and the federal bureaucracy in making and administering public policy, and because these elected and appointed officials draw their power from other sources and different constituencies, the President's task is to persuade these officials that it is in their own best interest to follow his lead. No wonder Mr. Truman recognized that effective presidential power is the power to influence other men rather than the power to command them. This in turn depends to a significant degree upon the personal qualities of the President. Few Washington observers thought that Harry S. Truman, upon his elevation to the presidency after Roosevelt's death, had the personal qualities necessary to exert strong leadership. But they underestimated "the man from Independence." To their surprise, Truman soon demonstrated a sure touch for the levers of presidential power. Not only did Truman make effective use of the status and formal powers of the President, but he also knew where the pressure points were in others and how to play on their needs and desires.

Sometimes a President must perform the role of negotiator to strengthen his bargaining position. If necessary, he can marshal public opinion behind him through presidential press conferences and nationwide telecasts. Mr. Truman played these trump cards with considerable skill—far better than his successor, Eisenhower.

During most of Eisenhower's eight years in office, the retired general was handicapped by his difficulty in understanding the nature of presidential power. Neustadt has commented on Ike's handling of his presidential duties: "Apparently he could not quite absorb the notion that effective power had to be extracted out of men's self-interest; neither did he quite absorb the notion that nobody else's interest could be wholly his own." [30]

Although the President's policy alternatives are generally limited to those for which he can mobilize support, he can also rely on patronage (the power to make government appointments on a basis other than merit alone) to win approval of his programs. Patronage is a chief executive's stock-in-trade for influencing the individual legislator's vote. In return for the lawmaker's support, the President can offer him or her a voice in the selection of an appointee to office; consideration of his or her state or district in the allocation of public works projects, space installations, or government contracts; and even the exertion of administrative discretionary authority in matters affecting a legislator's constituents before public agencies.[31]

No President ever dispensed office more lavishly than Abraham Lincoln. More recently, Woodrow Wilson, Franklin D. Roosevelt, and John F. Kennedy all found it expedient to withhold the loaves and fishes of federal patronage from partisans in Congress, pending action by them on the chief executive's key measures.

Despite these powers, the President must sometimes spend long hours reasoning, sparring, cajoling, and compromising with the rival centers of power—especially with the reluctant lawmakers on Capitol Hill. His bargaining power stems not only from the dispensation of patronage but also from his professional reputation and his popular prestige. It is also derived from the opinions of other men regarding his skill and from their appraisal of how the general public views him. In the final analysis, the use of presidential power depends upon the President's role performance—"his sense of power and of purpose and his own sense of self-confidence." But there are boundaries beyond which even the President cannot step, as President Nixon discovered in the wake of the Watergate affair.

The View from Capitol Hill

Since the President forced Congress out of the dominant leadership position early in the twentieth century, the lawmakers have experienced frequent periods of frustration, followed by long intervals of apathy and weariness. Although members of Congress may rightfully feel that they are the "first branch" of the government, the lawmakers have watched a series of Presidents preempt policy-making and decision-making roles while the legislators have remained on the sidelines.

From time to time, temper outbursts by individual senators and congressmen from both parties over their subordinate status have been heard on the floor of Congress and occasionally in print. Senator Abraham Ribicoff (D.-Conn.), for example, complained bitterly in 1964 that Congress "has surrendered its rightful leadership in the law-making process to the White House." The legislative branch, he wrote, "now merely filters legislative proposals from the President. . . . These days no one expects Congress to devise important bills. Instead, the legislative views of the President dominate the press, the public and Congress itself." [32]

Until the late 1960's, however, the periodic waves of congressional frustration over White House domination usually subsided as the legislators returned to "business as usual"—approving with slight alterations executive-drafted departmental budgets, sorting out the numerous executive-sponsored bills, overseeing in routine fashion the operations of the various "independent" agencies, and occasionally conducting an investigation of the executive branch. In the recent words of one White House critic, Senator Jacob Javits (R.-N.Y.):

> For too long we in Congress tended to take our cues from the other end of Pennsylvania Avenue [and] we waited, if not for instruction, certainly for direction and the direction was well on the way to becoming dictation.[33]

Early in the 1970's, however, Congress underwent a revitalization. Why this change? Several reasons have been advanced to explain the new "fighting attitude" of Congress. The failure of President Nixon to quickly de-escalate American involvement in the Vietnam War was a major factor. Congress, reflecting the public's attitude, grew increasingly disenchanted with the unending casualty lists as the war dragged on. Although the American commanders had repeatedly predicted that the United States "would soon see the light at the end of the tunnel," the Vietnamese cease-fire was not signed until January, 1973—and not until after the heavy American bombings of Hanoi and Haiphong had generated a tidal wave of disapproval throughout the free world. Subsequent bombings of Cambodian rebel forces finally exhausted Congress' patience with President Nixon's Indochina policy during the summer of 1973. Congress, relying on its infrequently used power of the purse, halted the use of all funds for these bombing missions on August 15, 1973.

Another reason for the resurgence of Congress was President Nixon's impoundment of over $12 billion in funds already appropriated by Congress in 1972-73. This action infuriated lawmakers in both parties. Congressional reaction led to the passage of legislation—the Congressional Budget and Impoundment Control Act of 1974—that deprives the President of the authority to withhold appropriated funds in the future. Also, President Nixon's repeated goading of Congress for its "free-spending habits" and unconcern for exceeding budget ceilings prompted Congress to pass legislation that establishes a joint congressional committee on budget and expenditures. This legislation will lessen the

Official Portrait of the United States Senate, December 10, 1971

Credit: National Geographic Photographer Courtesy U.S. Capitol Historical Society

President's heretofore dominant influence over the budget and enable Congress to impose its own ceilings on expenditures and coordinate revenue needs with spending limits. More is said about congressional budget reform in Chapter 6.

Thus, toward the end of the first Nixon Administration, Congress emerged from its shell of apathy and indolence to reassert its rightful role as a coequal branch of the federal government.

Shortly after Mr. Nixon's second inauguration the shock waves from the Watergate investigations helped reinforce congressional determination to recapture decision-making power that, in truth, had belonged to the lawmakers all along. The house impeachment inquiry into Mr. Nixon's conduct that followed the Watergate disclosures further accelerated congressional moves to restore a basic constitutional balance between the executive and legislative branches. It is, of course, too early to say whether the lawmakers will continue to reassert their constitutional prerogatives now that the Watergate scandals and the Nixon impeachment proceedings have concluded. But it seems fair to state that the country is moving closer to the constitutional balance of power envisaged by the framers than at any other time in the past century.

This still leaves a related question unanswered: Can Congress be the tribune of the people?

Congress: Tribune of the People?

Classic democratic theory assigns the greatest power to the legislative branch. Indeed, the British Parliament conducted its first skirmishes in the democratic revolution against the dominance of the Crown. Understandably, the early democratic theorists devoted their most eloquent arguments to justify the legitimacy of the legislative power. John Locke, the seventeenth-century English "natural rights" theorist, termed the legislative power "that which has a right to direct how the force of the commonwealth, shall be employed for preserving community and members of it." [34] The philosophical godfather of the founding fathers, Locke insisted that the legislature was the "supreme power of the commonwealth." Despite this strong philosophical defense of the legislative power, the framers made some major alterations on Locke's doctrine when they drafted the new governing document. Though the framers viewed the colonial legislatures as champions of the people against the power of the Crown, their recent experience with the Continental Congress and the Articles of Confederation forcefully suggested that representative assemblies were weak instruments for conducting foreign affairs or waging wars. That the legislative branch was ill equipped to deal with the public's daily problems during the pre-Constitution period has been expressed by a number of scholars. Louis Fisher comments:

> The framers shared a desire for greater efficiency and more reliable governmental machinery. Direct experience with state government and the Continental Congress convinced them of the need for a separate executive and inter-departmental checks. Chief among their concerns was the need to protect against legislative usurpations and to preserve the independence of the executive and judicial branches. Those were the dominant thoughts behind the separation of powers, not the doctrine of Montesquieu, fear of executive power, or a basic distrust of government. If the framers had wanted weak government they could have had that with the Articles of Confederation.[35]

James Madison, one of the coauthors of the *Federalist Papers,* argued that legislatures in a republic are more prone to tyranny than narrowly restrained executives. The architects of the early state constitutions, he stated, "seem never to have recollected the danger from legislative usurpation which by assembling all power in the same hands, must lead to the same tyranny as is threatened by executive usurpations." [36] Even Thomas Jefferson, the author of the Declaration of Independence, wrote in his *Notes on Virginia,* "173 despots would surely be as oppressive as one." [37]

To obtain the best of both worlds; that is, to protect the voice of the people and to provide executive direction to the ship of state, the authors of the Constitution decided to sacrifice the role of Congress as tribune of the people in favor of a separation of powers doctrine that divided executive leadership and law making. The founding fathers also came up with the ingenious solution that the three branches of the national government should be "so far connected and blended, as to give to each a *Constitutional* control over the others." [38] The American political system, then, represents a blending and mingling of powers—a structure based upon interdependence. Richard E. Neustadt has described it as "a government of separated institutions sharing powers." [39]

If powers are to be shared, disputes may arise over the division of powers and over which branch is to exercise authority in particular spheres of the government. Therefore, this question may be legitimately asked: Do shared institutional powers produce deadlock?

Presidential-Congressional Deadlock?

It would appear that the American separation of powers system puts the President and Congress on a collision course frequently. Actually, the historical record shows that the periods of stalemate between the White House and Capitol Hill have been infrequent—even when one major party has occupied the White House and the rival party has controlled Congress. During the period of 1952–1972, for example, the presidency and Congress were controlled by opposite parties for 12 of the 20 years. Yet the number of instances of presidential-congressional deadlock (see Table 3.1) during the Eisenhower terms and the first Nixon Administration, as evidenced by the number of presidential vetoes, was lower than during FDR's three full terms, when his party controlled both houses of Congress.

Warren Weaver, Jr., has pointed out that even President Truman's running battle with the so-called "Do Nothing" 80th Congress in 1948 and, to a lesser extent, with the 81st Congress, was marked by

TABLE 3.1 **Comparison of Presidential Vetoes During Roosevelt, Eisenhower, and Nixon Administrations (1933–45, 1953–61, 1969–72)**

	Vetoes	Vetoes Overridden
Roosevelt (1933–1945)	631	9
Eisenhower (1953–1961)	181	2
Nixon (1969–1972)	28	4

Sources: C. Herman Pritchett, *The American Constitution*, 2nd ed. (New York: McGraw-Hill), 1968, p. 332.
John H. Ferguson and Dean E. McHenry, *The American Federal Government*, 7th ed. (New York: McGraw Hill, 1963), p. 318.
"Nixon's Vetoes," *Congressional Quarterly*, Vol. XXX (Nov. 4, 1972), p. 2911.

. . . an extraordinary period of foreign policy cooperation between Congress and the White House and between the political parties within Congress. It produced the United Nations Charter ratification, regional security alliances, the Marshall Plan, the Truman Doctrine, and finally, even united support for the intervention in Korea.[40]

Two Presidencies

Aaron Wildavsky has suggested that we really have one President and two presidencies.[41] Other writers have also pointed out that in defense and foreign policy the President is in command and Congress takes a back seat. But in domestic policy no President has half as much power as he needs, while Congress is often in control. This mixture of concern and control over these two broad policy areas is illustrated by a remark made by Richard Nixon to author Theodore H. White in 1968: "I've always thought this country could run itself domestically, without a President. . . . You need a President for foreign policy . . . the President makes foreign policy." [42]

Once in office, recent Presidents have displayed an overriding concern with foreign affairs that often puts domestic policy on the back burner. Arthur M. Schlesinger, Jr., recalls that President Kennedy "in the first two months of his administration probably spent more time on Laos than on anything else." When Secretary of the Interior Udall attempted to talk with Kennedy about natural resources, Udall stated in exasperation, "He's imprisoned by Berlin." [43] Lyndon Johnson, in November, 1963, immediately following President Kennedy's funeral and with tears still on his face, talked with U.S. Ambassador to Vietnam Henry Cabot Lodge and made his first major decision as President, stating categorically, "I am not going to lose Vietnam. I am not going to be the President who saw Southeast Asia go the way China went." [44] Recent history shows that except for a flurry of Great Society legislation in 1965, the Vietnam War consumed most of Johnson's time as President. Nixon, in his first 100 days as President, reaffirmed his aforementioned remark about the high priority of foreign affairs by meeting with the National Security Council 15 times and the joint congressional leadership only three times.

Prior to the Vietnam War, during the cold war years, Presidents rarely had major setbacks in controlling foreign policy. A partial list of presidential victories is indeed impressive: entry into the United Nations; the "Truman Doctrine," which became the cornerstone of the American postwar policy of containing Communist expansion; the Marshall Plan to rebuild Europe; the North Atlantic Treaty committing the United States to the defense of western Europe; and the "Eisenhower Doctrine" of 1957, which received congressional support by a joint resolution that read in part: "if the President determines the necessity," the United States is "prepared to use armed forces to assist" any friendly Middle Eastern country.

Of all presidential proposals for legislation in foreign and defense policy from 1948 to 1964, Presidents prevailed 70 percent of the time.[45] It may also be noted that President Nixon took a position on 33 foreign affairs and defense roll-call votes in 1972, and lost only one-third of the time. This was during an election year when the President's use of prerogatives in foreign affairs was being questioned by an opposition Congress, and voters had become disenchanted with the war in Southeast Asia.

On the other hand, Presidents have not fared as well in their domestic legislative proposals. Indeed, Presidents have often been frustrated by Congress. Presidential successes in domestic legislation occur infrequently—usually during periods of economic crises or national emergencies. During the period of 1948-1964 Presidents were successful with only 40 percent of 2499 domestic proposals. President Franklin D. Roosevelt's New Deal triumphs in the 1930's and the landslide victory of Lyndon Johnson in 1964, both accompanied by large Democratic majorities in Congress, mark the few times when Presidents have had major successes with their domestic programs. Wildavsky concludes:

> From 1938, when conservatives regrouped their forces, to the time of his death, Franklin Roosevelt did not get a single piece of significant domestic legislation passed. Truman lost out on most of his intense domestic preferences, except perhaps for housing. Sure Eisenhower did not ask for much domestic legislation, he did not meet consistent defeat yet he failed in his general policy of curtailing government commitments. Kennedy, of course, faced great difficulties with domestic legislation.[46]

Franklin D. Roosevelt was successful in obtaining sweeping legislation during his first "one hundred days" in order to handle the economic crisis facing the nation. With the depression still gripping the nation and nearly 40 percent of the blue-collar workers still without jobs, Roosevelt complained to his advisor, Thomas Corcoran: "You know, in this business, you must remem-

TABLE 3.2 **Presidential Box Scores: 1954–70**

President, Year		Number of proposals submitted	Number approved by Congress	Percent approved
Eisenhower	1954	232	150	65
	1955	207	96	46
	1956	225	103	46
	1957	206	76	37
	1958	234	110	47
	1959	228	93	41
	1960	183	56	31
Kennedy	1961	355	172	48
	1962	298	133	45
Kennedy-Johnson	1963	401	109	27
Johnson	1964	217	125	58
	1965	469	323	69
	1966	371	207	56
	1967	431	205	48
	1968	414	231	56
Nixon	1969	171	53	32
	1970	210	97	46

Source: William C. Mitchell, *Why Vote* (Chicago: Markham Publishing Company, 1971), p. 120.

ber Ty Cobb. If you bat .400, you're a champion." [47] Table 3.2 indicates the overall legislative successes of recent Presidents. The truism of FDR's statement is indicated by the many years in which Presidents have not done much better than .400 at the plate. In addition, some of these "victories" have been based upon bills that were noncontroversial in nature.

Why are Presidents so much more successful in foreign affairs than in domestic policy making? Part of the reason may be that the world has changed more rapidly than the nation. For example, the number of nation-states increased from 53 in 1939 to 135 in 1973. Israel did not exist as a state in 1946, nor were India, Pakistan, or Indonesia independent states at that time. Most of the nation-states of Africa still had colonial status as late as 1958.

Technological breakthroughs during and after World War II made weapons systems obsolete almost as soon as they were off the drawing board. A miscalculation during an international crisis, such as the Cuban missile crisis, could have led to a nuclear holocaust. The contemporary world requires instant decisions in response to the threat of aggression. Presidential judgments can mean the difference between war and peace. Thus, when the President acts in international affairs, he finds his action viewed as important for the world and his decision irreversible. As President Kennedy remarked, "Domestic policy . . . can only defeat us, foreign policy can kill us." [48] World events have thus created a need for executive leadership.

Until recently, Congress has been willing to step aside and defer to the President in foreign policy. But in the field of domestic policy Congress has more than held its own against the President over the years. Indeed, one might say that Congress exercises a "legislative veto" over many White House domestic proposals. Why? One reason is that congressmen respond to the pleas and pressures of a wide variety of interest groups that are deeply concerned about domestic issues but much less interested in foreign affairs. Generally, White House domestic proposals obtain congressional approval only after extensive White House lobbying and after the various interest groups have been placated. This congressional "obstacle course" causes many domestic proposals to be blocked or stalled until such time that enough congressmen and senators, responding to the dominant interest groups in their constituencies, believe that the proposal enjoys the support of a majority of the voters.

Because it recognizes the need for speed in foreign affairs, Congress has been—at least until recently—much more willing to delegate authority to the President in external matters. But in domestic policy Congress feels that it has as much (and sometimes more) information available as the executive branch to make sound decisions. There always have been and always will be groups of legislators who know more about a single agency or domestic program than the chief executive. Thus, the tax "experts" or the energy "experts" on Capitol Hill see little need to defer to the President or his spokesmen when drafting domestic legislation on these subjects.

Over the years, Congress has been underrated as an innovator and an agency for leadership. One study made in the 1940's showed that Congress had exhibited more leadership in policy making than had the President. In a detailed study of 90 major laws in ten categories spanning the period from 1890 to 1940, Lawrence Chamberlain concluded:

> the President could be given credit for approximately 20 percent, the Congress for about 40 percent; thirty percent were the product of both the President and Congress, and less than 10 percent of external pressure groups.[49]

Of the 90 laws, 77 originated from bills that did not have the sponsorship of the White House, Chamberlain found that while legislation represented a joint effort, Congress had in general tended to be more aggressive and innovative than the executive branch.

Time and space do not permit a detailed analysis of an updated version of Chamberlain's ten major categories of legislation, but a brief sample of postwar legislation in one or two fields will lend further support to his thesis. Technology, for example, a field requiring an expertise more likely to be found in the executive agencies than Congress (so it is widely claimed), has received more attention from lawmakers than from the President. Since 1945 Congress has passed three major acts to deal with technological breakthroughs in atomic energy, space technology, and satellite communications. In all three cases Congress has been an equal or dominant partner in the establishment of new agencies. For example, the Atomic Energy Act of 1946 has been largely credited to the late Senator Brien McMahon and his committee.[50] Nor has congressional interest in atomic energy policy declined since the establishment of the Atomic Energy Commission. Lawmakers have kept a watchful eye on atomic energy policy through the Joint Committee on Atomic Energy—probably the most powerful committee in the nation's history. As a policy maker, the Joint Committee has often dominated the Atomic Energy Commission.

A decade later, Congress reacted quickly to the Soviet-launched sputnik by passing legislation to establish an organization to conduct a national program in outer space—the National Aeronautics and Space Act of 1958. Four years later, Congress prodded a rather reluctant executive branch into action that resulted in the Communications Satellite Act of 1962. As Moe and Teel put it, "Congress, through its repeated investigations, established the basic public record, sharpened the relevant issues, and provided a marketplace of ideas with all interested groups being given a chance to present their cases." [51]

Shared Leadership

Despite the distinction that Congress usually makes between presidential handling of foreign and domestic policies, the President and Congress have for the most part developed a compatible working relationship over the years. This has happened even during periods of divided government; that is, when one major party has controlled the White House and the rival party, the Congress. Until the Watergate scandal, President Nixon and the Democratic-controlled Congress often agreed on a number of issues—the defense budget, farm legislation, social security benefits, and taxation policies.

This duality of leadership, first espoused by the framers of the Constitution, almost doubles the capacity for representation in our system. The electorate is offered two channels of political input—presidential and congressional—"for the price of one." Over the years this dual system has often drawn the two branches of government toward greater accommodation with each other, despite a formal separation of powers.

In reassessing the separation of powers doctrine, Ralph Huitt commented some years ago that

> The Founding Fathers were, above all else, practical men; they were not so much interested in a scientific separation of

powers as they were in drawing on the lessons of experience to make a workable structure for the future. . . . At the same time, they softened the separation with checks and balances . . . and left their equally pragmatic descendents largely free to distribute and share powers as current exigencies seemed to require.[52]

One team of authors has observed recently: "The Framers relied on self-restraint to keep each branch of government from too much interference in the responsibilities of others."[53] Under their new constitutional system, the checks and balances were supposed to operate automatically. But, in fact, they have not. Although history tells us that the power center in our federal government has shifted between the White House and Capitol Hill at irregular intervals, the twentieth century has been a period of almost uninterrupted aggrandizement by the presidency. As power has gravitated to the White House, Presidents have been less and less inclined to accept self-restraint in dealing with Congress. Instead, they have been acting more and more like "emperor-kings," determining national priorities with only perfunctory consultation with Congress. In recent years, several chief executives have engaged secretly in foreign military interventions to a degree never dreamed of by the founding fathers. Fortunately, from their study of ancient history the authors of the Constitution concluded that the single most effective means of preventing despotic rule was the division of the reins of power.

By vesting in Congress the power of the purse and the right to conduct investigations of the executive branch, the framers assured the legislative branch that opportunities for leadership would always be available for those with the courage to accept and counter executive challenges. As the current resurgence of Congress has demonstrated, the concept of shared power remains as viable a blueprint for joint presidential-legislative leadership today as it was for the founding fathers during that hot summer of 1787 in Philadelphia, where they produced the final draft of the Constitution.

UNEASY PARTNERS: CONGRESS AND THE PRESIDENT IN FOREIGN AFFAIRS

It may be said that the Constitution established a government of separate institutions sharing power. The reins of power in the conduct of American foreign policy have been exercised dramatically by the President of the United States, especially since World War II. In discussing his role in foreign affairs, Harry S. Truman declared emphatically: "I make American foreign policy." The view of presidential dominance in this realm received early support from Thomas Jefferson, who stated that the conduct of foreign affairs is "executive altogether." The Supreme Court added legitimacy to this position by holding in *United States* v. *Curtiss-Wright Export Corporation* (1936) that the President had authority vested in him not only by a delegation of power from Congress but that "the exclusive power of the President as *sole* organ of the federal government in the field of International Relations is a power which does not require as its basis an act of Congress." [1]

In recent years this view of presidential dominance in foreign affairs has suffered by the disillusionment of the public and Congress with the conduct of the United States' longest undeclared war, the war in Vietnam. This switch in attitude is reflected in the change in the view of the Chairman of the Senate Foreign Relations Committee, J. William Fulbright (D.-Ark.), who stated in the late 1950's that "for the existing requirements of American foreign policy we have hobbled the President by too niggardly a grant of power." [2] By 1972 his views had been altered drastically; he then concluded that "it may not be too much to say that as far as foreign policy is concerned, our governmental system is no longer one of separate powers but rather one of elected, executive dictatorship." [3]

Constitutional Division

The Constitution does not neglect the conduct of foreign policy; indeed, its often ambiguous language has set the stage for the encroachments of one branch upon the other. The late Edward S. Corwin, in his classic study of the American presidency, observed that "The Constitution, considered only for its affirmative grants of powers which are capable of affecting the issue, is an invitation to struggle for the privilege of directing American foreign policy." [4] When charges are made that there has been a great usurpation of powers by recent Presidents or that the Congress is obstructing the President's conduct of foreign affairs, authorities will often turn to the specific grants of power that each branch received under the Constitution in order to justify their arguments.

The framers vested most of the federal government's enumerated powers in foreign affairs in the legislative branch. Provisions in Article I include the powers to declare war; to grant letters of marque and reprisal; to make rules concerning captures on land and water; to raise and support armies; to provide and maintain a navy; to make rules for the government and regulate the land and naval forces; to call forth the militia to execute the laws of the Union, suppress insurrections, and repel invasions; and to organize, arm, and discipline the militia. In addition to these listed or "enumerated" powers, Congress is given the power to make laws which are "necessary and proper" to carry into effect these specific powers (Article I, Section 8, Clause 18—the elastic clause).

On the other hand, Article II provides that the President shall be commander-in-chief of the army and the navy of the United States, and of the militia of the several states, when called into actual service of the United States; that he shall have power to make treaties, provided two-thirds of the senators present concur; that he shall nominate ambassadors, and by and with the advice and consent of the Senate, shall appoint them, as well as other public ministers and consuls; and that he shall receive ambassadors and other public ministers. Presidents have also pointed to their own "elastic clause," Article II, Section 1, which grants to the President "the executive power of the United States," to gain a greater voice in conducting foreign affairs.

It should be clear from this statement of enumerated powers that the Congress has more expressed powers delegated to it under the Constitution than does the executive. If we restrict executive power in foreign affairs to specific constitutional grants, then the office of the President is indeed narrow in scope. Most Presidents, however, have refused to view their powers so narrowly. For example, Presidents have viewed the commander-in-chief clause not merely as an office or title but as a means of commanding the armed forces. Thus, when President Nixon employed the armed forces in Cambodia and Laos for the purpose of protecting American lives, he interpreted his commander-in-chief powers in the broadest scope. Likewise, Lincoln expanded his expressed powers when he initiated wartime measures after the southern states had seceded from the Union. He pointed to the oath of office which requires the President to preserve, protect, and defend the Constitution. These examples illustrate how far Presidents have expanded their powers by inferring from clearly delegated constitutional powers the broad powers necessary to carry out their expressed powers.

"Inherent powers" are those which the presidency has claimed by virtue of the fact that as the chief executive office of the United States, the office includes powers in foreign affairs which need not be expressed or implied. Justice Sutherland, speaking for the Supreme Court in *United States* v. *Curtiss-Wright* (1936), stated that "The President alone has the power to speak or listen as the representative of the nation" and that in international affairs the President has "a degree of discretion and freedom from statutory restriction that would not be admissible were domestic affairs alone involved." Since the *Curtiss-Wright* decision, Presidents have repeatedly referred to this seemingly boundless grant of authority given to the President in international affairs.

The Treaty-Making Powers

Nowhere is the jockeying for position and conflict for control over foreign affairs more forcefully exhibited than in the treaty-making process. The founding fathers were well aware of the fact that the British monarch could conclude treaties solely on his own initiative. Dissatisfied with this arrangement, as well as with Article VI of the Articles of Confederation (which had granted sole control over the conduct of foreign affairs to Congress), the authors of the Constitution provided that the President would be required to seek the advice and consent of two-thirds of the Senate before making binding commitments, in the form of treaties, with other nations. According to Article VI of the U.S. Constitution, treaties conforming to the powers of national government and under the authority of the United States shall be the supreme law of the land and thus enforceable in the courts. Treaties, laws passed in pursuance of treaties, and executive orders issued to carry treaties into effect are as binding on citizens as are all laws passed by the national government. Citizens who fearfully remembered the powers exercised in foreign affairs by the British monarch as the "sole" and "absolute" representative of the nation were assured by Alexander Hamilton in the 69th essay of the *Federalist Papers* that "the one can do alone what the other can do only with the concurrence of a branch of the legislature." It was assumed that the President and the Senate would work in close collaboration on both the negotiation and ratification stages of treaty making. This cooperation envisioned by the farmers occurred only for a brief time—and from George Washington's point of view, unsatisfactorily.

In August, 1789, Washington met with senators to secure their advice and consent on an Indian treaty. The senators, fearing that the father of the nation would dominate their deliberations, excused the President and continued their discussion of the treaty in private. Although the Senate subsequently approved the treaty, the experience convinced Washington, who had been humiliated by the Senate's impolite treatment, that consultation with the Senate on treaties was ill advised. The result was that the Senate asserted its independence by separating its functions from those of the President, while he accepted this separation in order to maintain his power over treaty making. Thus, the first effort at cooperation and collaboration by the executive and the legislature at all stages of treaty making "in the spirit of an executive council" (as Woodrow Wilson once put it), convinced Washington and future Presidents that the function of the Senate must be restricted to confirming the negotiators and approving or rejecting the treaty draft.[5]

Congressional confirmation of treaty negotiators occurred only during the early decades of the Republic. Washington, in nominating Jay to negotiate a treaty with Great Britain, Adams, in negotiations with France, Jefferson, in negotiations for the Louisiana Purchase, and Madison, in the Treaty of Ghent, submitted the names of the negotiators prior to their negotiations. This practice ended after 1815, and in the last 150 years Presidents have felt free to name whomever they wished to serve as negotiators.

Thus, personal presidential consultation and the power to confirm commissioners to negotiate treaties had slipped from the hands of the Senate during the early years of the Republic. This lapse of power has been confirmed as a permanent loss by the Supreme Court. In the *Curtiss-Wright* case Justice Sutherland asserted that "he [the President] alone negotiates . . . into the field of negotiations the Senate cannot intrude."[6] This power has been reaffirmed by scholars such as Edward S. Corwin who stated, "It is today established that the President alone has power to negotiate treaties with foreign governments."[7] By its own actions the Senate has reinforced this precedent. In the Versailles negotiations following World War I, for example, some senate Republicans proposed sending eight Republican senators to Paris to acquaint themselves with the peace negotiations. No action was taken by the Senate on this proposal. One Republican senator, former diplomat Henry White, attended the conference at the invitation of President Wilson, but he played no role as a senate spokesman and, in fact, had little role in the negotiations.

The relationship between executive and legislature in this twilight zone of treaty consultation has evolved into separate institutions which exercise separate powers rather than separate institutions which share powers. The power of the Senate to accept, reject, or amend treaties is acknowledged as a rightful power. By no means has the Senate failed to exercise this power of life and death over treaties. In light of the Senate's rejection of the Treaty of Versailles, few Presidents have chosen to completely ignore written or representative consultation with the Senate in treaty making. Presidents have deemed it wise on occasion to involve key senators in the negotiating process. Thus, President Franklin D. Roosevelt selected Senators Tom Connally (D.-Tex.) and Arthur Vandenberg (R.-Mich.) to be members of the United States delegation to the San Francisco conference in 1945 which negotiated the United Nations charter. More recently, President Kennedy chose a panel of senators to participate in the 1963 nuclear test ban treaty negotiations. Senator Everett Dirksen (R.-Ill.), the minority leader of the Republican party, played a key role in its passage by advising President Kennedy to assure the Senate that he would not de deterred from maintaining a vigorous weapons system and that he would not alter the treaty except by employing the treaty-making procedure.[8]

In 1868 the Senate strengthened its own hand by voting to change its standing rules to allow reservations and amendments to treaties to be submitted by mere majority vote. Before 1900 over 80 treaties had been altered by the Senate in some way. One-third of these draft treaties either failed ratification or were abandoned by the President as not acceptable. According to one author, *no* important treaties were ratified between 1871 and 1892.[9] This practice has continued in the twentieth century to the extent that, as one source notes, in the first quarter of this century, "58 proposed treaties were changed by the Senate; 40 percent of them were abandoned or discarded by the President as no longer in the national interest." [10]

Woodrow Wilson characterized the treaty-making power as

the "treaty-marring power," while John Hay, summing up his bitter experience as McKinley's secretary of state, remarked that "A treaty entering the Senate is like a bull going into the arena. No one can say just how and when the final blow will fall. But one thing is certain—it will never leave the arena alive." [11]

An editorial in the *New York Times* of March 10, 1967, seemed to imply that it is irresponsible for the Senate to change the terms of a negotiated treaty. The *Times* commented as follows:

> A treaty is a contract negotiated by the executive branch with the government of one of more other countries. In the process there is normally hard bargaining and the final result usually represents a compromise in which everyone has made concessions. Thus when the Senate adds amendments or reservations to a treaty it is unilaterally changing the terms of a settled bargain. The practical effect of such action is really to reopen the negotiations and force the other party or parties to reexamine their previously offered approval.
>
> Every time the Senate exercises this privilege it necessarily casts doubt upon the creditability of the President and his representatives and weakens the bargaining power of the United States in the international arena.

Under the Constitution, treaties brought to the Senate for its consent are only tentative bargains. To treat them as settled bargains is to further strip a constitutional function from that body. Presidents do not come to consult the Senate but to brief it and receive its support on the dotted line of the contract.

Some senators are attempting to reestablish a major role for the Senate prior to the treaty ratification stage. Senator Vance Hartke (D.-Ind.) introduced a senate resolution in July, 1971, which stipulates that "no treaty may be constitutionally negotiated by the President without the prior advice of the Senate. . . ." [12] The see-saw between the executive and Senate over treaty making is likely to continue to be one of the unsettled points of tension between the White House and Capitol Hill.

Frequent senate action to withhold ratification or to reserve its consent has accelerated presidential attempts to circumvent the formal treaty as a means of conducting foreign affairs. Instead, Presidents have developed two major ploys to bypass the Senate and commit the United States to their foreign policies: use of joint resolutions (or legislative acts) and executive agreements.

In 1844 President Tyler attempted to bring Texas into the Union by submitting a treaty of annexation to the Senate. The Senate demanded information about troop deployment, and after receiving this information acted quickly to reject the treaty. This did not deter Tyler, who proposed an alternative: annexation by joint resolution. This was quickly passed by a majority in both houses. Thus, by annexing Texas in 1845 via a joint resolution, Congress placed another weapon in the hands of the presidency. After the Senate defeated a treaty to annex Hawaii in 1898, the Congress voted by joint resolution to annex this territory.

In January, 1955, President Eisenhower sought and received a joint resolution from Congress to use American armed forces in the event of a Communist attack on Formosa or the Pescadores Islands. In 1961 President Kennedy asked for and received a joint resolution from Congress in support of his efforts to ensure Allied access rights to West Berlin.

After a reported North Vietnamese PT boat attack on U.S. destroyers off the coast of Vietnam, President Johnson asked for approval of the "Tonkin Gulf Resolution" on August 4, 1964. On the third day after receiving the presidential request, Congress, by a vote of 88 to 2 in the Senate and 416 to 0 in the House of Representatives, authorized the President "to take all necessary steps, including the use of force" to repel aggression in Southeast Asia. Presidents have found the joint resolution a useful tool to gain congressional support for entering into foreign military operations without a formal declaration of war.

In light of Secretary of States Dulles' "pactomania" of the 1950's—SEATO, CENTO, and so forth—one might argue that these commitments would have received the support of two-thirds of the Senate needed to ratify all treaties. But these actions do not weaken the conclusion that the treaty-making power of the Senate has been severely eroded by congressional as well as presidential actions.[12] Clearly, Presidents have used these resolutions to avoid public controversy by involving the Congress in the responsibility for foreign relations without meaningful congressional consultations or control over the conduct of foreign relations. Truman's failure to seek and receive a congressional resolution in support of his policies in the Korean War may have led to controversy that other Presidents would like to avoid. Thus, congressional resolutions in support of presidential actions are often not just a formality for the President but a device for his political convenience.

Executive Agreements

Executive agreements are one of the devices employed most often by Presidents to circumvent the use of the Senate's veto power over treaties. Thus, in 1905, when the Senate refused to approve a treaty with Santo Domingo which would have placed its customhouses under American control, Theodore Roosevelt, as he himself described it, "put the agreement into effect, and I continued to execute it for two years before the Senate acted; and I would have continued it until the end of my term, if necessary, without any action by Congress." [13]

What are executive agreements? Is there a constitutional basis of power for entering into such commitments? Are they really used to circumvent the treaty-making power exercised by the Senate? How has Congress responded to their use?

Executive agreements are agreements entered into by the executive branch of government with foreign nations without the necessity of direct action by the Congress. When Senator Guy Gillette (D.-Iowa) requested the State Department to clarify the difference between executive agreements and treaties, it replied "that a treaty was something they had to send to the Senate to get approval by two-thirds vote. An executive agreement was something they did not have to send to the Senate." Reportedly, this reminded the senator of his youth on an Iowa farm. He had asked the hired man how to tell the difference between male and female pigeons. The answer was, "You put a piece of corn in front of the pigeon. If he picks it up, it is a he; if she picks it up, it is a she." [14] Another attempt to distinguish between agreements and treaties is to say that treaties involve long-range commitments, while agreements are short lived or fulfilled by a single act. Still another attempt to distinguish treaties from executive agreements is to say that treaties are designed to involve the United States in major political commitments, and executive agreements are designed for routine, day-to-day, nonpolitical commitments. Both of these distinctions are questionable and we will return to them after considering the constitutional bases for executive agreements.

Executive agreements have as much force under domestic and international law as do treaties made under the authority given to the national government by the Constitution. Justice Sutherland, speaking for the Supreme Court in *United States* v. *Belmont* (1937), laid to rest any question that executive agreements may have less constitutional validity than treaties and placed them on an equal footing. In Justice Sutherland's emphatic opinion he states flatly that "In respect of what was done here [Franklin D. Roosevelt's 1933 executive agreement establishing diplomatic relations with the Soviet Union], the *Executive* had authority to speak as the *sole* organ of that [national] government." [15] An executive agreement is as much the law of the land as a treaty, and in the *Belmont* case the Supreme Court held that it prevails over conflicting state laws.

Executive agreements are generally of one of three types: (a) those entered into pursuant to an existing treaty; (b) those entered into under legislation enacted by Congress; and (c) those entered into under the authority of the President granted him by the Constitution. According to a State Department spokesman, 97 percent of executive agreements are made pursuant to a treaty approved by the Senate or prior statutes approved by Congress.[16] In 1953 Secretary of State John Foster Dulles commented before a senate committee considering the proposed Bricker Amendment (which sought to curtail the use of executive agreements) that agreements were necessary to conduct the day-to-day business of foreign affairs. He claimed that about 10,000 minor executive agreements had been made in carrying into effect the NATO treaty alone.[17]

One example of an executive agreement made pursuant to existing legislation is the agreement between the United States and Canada which followed congressional enactment of a law authorizing the St. Lawrence seaway project in 1954. Interestingly, in 1934 the Senate had refused to ratify a treaty which would have permitted the building of the seaway.

Agreements entered into solely upon independent presidential authority without expressed statutory authority or pursuant to existing treaties are justified by constitutional clauses granting the President power as "commander-in-chief," "executive power," power "to receive ambassadors," and so forth. Included in this category are the exchange of "obsolescent" U.S. destroyers with Britain in 1940 in return for the lease of British bases in the Caribbean, and the Yalta and Potsdam agreements in 1945 which decided the control of conquered land following World War II.

It should be noted that the Supreme Court's broad interpretation of presidential discretion to enter into executive agreements has not been unlimited. Executive agreements directly contrary to congressional statutes are invalid.[18] Also, the Supreme Court has made it clear that the Constitution prevents agreements from impairing individual rights such as trial by jury.[19]

Those who consider executive agreements a device for circumventing the Senate's treaty-making role in foreign affairs are pleased that the extensive use of agreements (often without congressional knowledge of their existence) and the importance of agreements in committing our government to broad fields of action have led to efforts in Congress to curb the power of the executive. Table 4.1 indicates the increasing use of executive agreements. This trend has continued; the record of the Nixon Administration from January, 1969, to May, 1972, shows 71 treaties and 608 executive agreements.[20] By quantity alone there can be little doubt that executive agreements play a major role in the conduct of American foreign policy.

More importantly, of the 87 international compacts concluded during the first 50 years of the Republic, the 60 treaties were the

TABLE 4.1 **Treaties and Executive Agreements (1789–1970)**

Period	Treaties	Executive Agreements	Totals
1789–1839	60	27	87
1839–1889	215	238	453
1889–1939	524	917	1441
1940–1970	310	5653	5963
	1109	6835	7944

Source: Louis Fisher, *President and Congress* (New York: The Free Press, 1972), p. 45.

most significant foreign commitments. Items such as permitting the President to enter into international agreements involving postal exchanges were left to executive agreements under statutory authorization. But all this has changed in recent years, according to some presidential critics. The Senate is now being permitted to consider and asked to ratify a treaty with Brazil concerning shrimp and another with Mexico for "The Recovery of Returned or Stolen Archeological, Historical, and Cultural Property." On the other hand, Presidents from 1953 to the present have committed the United States to the defense of the Franco dictatorship in Spain by use of executive agreements. The view of those who feel that the Senate may have lost its primary role in treaty making because of the indiscriminate use of executive agreements has been summed up by one senator who remarked acidly in 1969, "We have come close to reversing the traditional distinction between the treaty as the instrument of a major commitment and the executive agreement as the instrument of a minor one." [21] Three years later, another senator complained about the function of ratifying a treaty "to preserve cultural artifacts in a friendly neighboring country at the same time the Chief Executive is moving American military men and material around the globe like so many pawns in a chess game." [22] These critics might also have examined President Lyndon Johnson's executive agreement with the Philippines in which the U.S. agreed to pay $35 million in cash to the Philippine government while it agreed to send 2200 noncombat troops to Vietnam under the guise of "volunteers." Similar agreements were made with South Korea and Thailand. In all three cases, the substances of these agreements were kept secret from the Congress. Recently, Senator Stuart Symington (D.-Mo.) also found that there were secret annexes to the agreement with Spain which had been kept from the Congress for nearly 20 years.[23]

Congressional Efforts to Curtail Executive Usurpation

As a result of widespread secret diplomacy by the White House, legislators have begun to reassert Congress' role in treaty making to prevent what many feel has become the abuse of the executive agreement. A preliminary effort in the early 1950's to control the use of the executive agreement was the so-called Bricker Amendment, which would have required executive agreements and treaties to either have implementing legislation or lack domestic authority. More recently, Senator Clifford Case of New Jersey introduced a bill to curb the use of executive agreements that circumvent the Senate's authority to advise and consent on treaties. In 1972, Congress passed a law requiring the State Department to transmit the lawmakers the text of all international agreements, other than treaties, within 60 days of their execution (Public Law 92–403). If the President deems the material in the agreement too sensitive for public disclosure, it goes to the Senate Foreign Relations Committee. (A similar bill had passed the Senate in 1954 but failed in the House because its sponsors neglected to provide benefits for members of that body.) The 1972 law will necessarily result in increased congressional knowledge of American commitments abroad; henceforth Congress will have the information necessary to make more reasoned judgments in international affairs.

Senator Sam Ervin (D.-N.C.) has proposed legislation which would give Congress the power to veto all executive agreements within 60 days by a concurrent resolution passed in both houses.

Senator Case has offered a second measure which would require that all agreements for military bases abroad be sent to the Senate as treaties. Some may question the wisdom of imposing the congressional machinery on the day-to-day operations of American foreign policy making. Critics insist, however, that the framers of the Constitution meant to reserve this aspect of international relations to the executive.

We concur with those who argue that the proper function of Congress is to deliberate and play a major role in deciding the purposes and objectives of American foreign policy. The shaping of American foreign policy should be a joint effort; the President should provide leadership and the Congress should articulate the values served by our foreign policy. J. William Fulbright, Chairman of the Senate Foreign Relations Committee, has argued that the proper role of Congress is to use the Foreign Relations Committee as a forum to discuss the direction of American foreign policy. It can do this rationally only with adequate information.[24] Recently, Congress has been encouraged to secure the needed information from concluded executive agreements to make reasoned judgments. The Senate floor can also serve as a forum to provide direction to the executive for its conduct of day-to-day operations of American foreign policy. However, we believe that Senator Ervin's bill would remove the flexibility the President needs to conduct regular intercourse with foreign governments. The Supreme Court, as previously noted, has ruled that when Congress passes legislation contravening an executive agreement, the legislation prevails. On the other hand, we see merit in the proposal of Senator Case to require the submission to the Senate of agreements establishing foreign military bases, since this directly commits the United States to the defense of the nation on whose soil these bases are located.

In the next chapter we turn our attention to foreign military commitments and deal with the issues of who decides when American soldiers go to war and what the proper role is for Congress and the President in today's world of nuclear weapons.

COMMANDER-IN-CHIEF OR CONGRESS: WHO MAKES WAR?

On October 22, 1962, President John Kennedy reported to a stunned American public that Soviet missile sites were being constructed in Cuba, which, if fired at American cities, could kill about 80 million Americans in less than twelve minutes. He ordered a naval blockade that evening which presented "the greatest danger of catastrophic war since the advent of the nuclear age."[1] Eleven years later, shortly after midnight on October 25, 1973, President Richard Nixon ordered American bases throughout the world to an alert status. This action was designed to warn the Soviet Union that the United States would not tolerate unilateral Soviet military intervention in the Middle East during the Yom Kippur War. These actions illustrate why two authors of a popular textbook on Congress begin with the phrase, "We are living in an executive-centered world."[2]

The President is more influential than Congress in making military policy, despite the recent congressional assertion of its coequal role in foreign military commitments by the passage of the 1973 War Powers Act. This new legislation to curtail presidential war-making activities is discussed in this chapter. In addition, this chapter covers the constitutional basis of this awesome concentration of powers in the presidency. We shall also explore other examples of how Congress is attempting to restrain the executive in war making.

Conflicting Theories of War-Making Powers

The costly American involvement in the Vietnamese conflict has painfully reminded Congress that its constitutional power to declare war has had little practical application in today's world. Congress has rarely exercised its power to declare war on its own initiative. When Congress has exercised this prerogative, it has been at the recommendation of the President, and usually it has been a recognition of an existing state of war. Only five of the eleven major foreign conflicts to which this nation has committed its armed forces for extended periods have been preceded by a declaration of war. Yet, according to figures compiled by the Library of Congress in 1970, the United States armed forces have been sent abroad 165 times to protect United States property, citizens, or interests.[3]

Despite the fact that provisions of the Constitution explicitly grant to Congress the power to declare war, raise and support armies, and provide and maintain naval forces, the actions of our Presidents—particularly recent Presidents—have been to concentrate in themselves almost complete discretion to exercise war powers. Presidents have unilaterally employed American forces abroad at least 125 times (according to figures compiled by the State Department) without authorization from the Congress. The State Department, in its defense of the Vietnam War, stated:

> Since the Constitution was adopted there have been at least 125 instances in which the President has ordered the armed forces to take action or maintain positions abroad without prior congressional authorization . . . the Constitution leaves to the President the judgment to determine whether the circumstances of a particular armed attack are so urgent and the potential consequences so threatening to the security of the United States that he should act without formally consulting Congress.[4]

Are such presidential acts constitutional? What are the powers of the President and Congress? Congressional actions, such as the 1964 Gulf of Tonkin Resolution and the acquiescence of Congress during the "police action" of the United States in the Dominican Republic in 1965, have reinforced the established practice of congressional subservience to the executive branch with respect to the war-making powers.

Article II, Section 2 of the Constitution provides that "the

President shall be Commander-in-Chief of the Army and Navy of the United States, and of the militia of the several states, when called into the actual service of the United States." The founding fathers debated the grant to Congress of the "sole" power to declare war and defeated a motion to strike this grant from the Constitution. In response to a suggestion by Pierce Butler of South Carolina that the President be given sole power to declare war, Elbridge Gerry of Massachusetts retorted that he "never expected to hear in a republic a motion to empower the Executive alone to declare war." [5]

Activist Presidents can point to additional constitutional powers in their oath of office "to preserve, protect, and defend the Constitution" and the inherent powers derived from the general heading "executive power" to expand and justify their war-making activities. Presidents have differed in their views on the proper role of Congress and the executive to initiate and carry out foreign military conflicts. To illustrate differing attitudes on war making, the positions and actions of three Presidents will now be examined.

Madison View

Our early Presidents indicated some reluctance to initiate military operations without prior congressional authorization. In 1801 Jefferson refused to allow the navy to attack the Tripoli pirates on the grounds that Congress had not declared war. In 1812 Madison proposed a declaration of war when British warships were attacking American vessels. His message to Congress reflected a view he had espoused as one of the founding fathers on the question of the war-making power:

> . . . on the side of Great Britain, a state of war against the United States exists; and on the side of the United States, a state of peace towards Great Britain exists. Whether the United States shall continue passive under the progressive usurpations . . . or, opposing force to force in defense of their national rights, shall commit a just cause into the hands of the

Almighty Disposer of events . . . is a solemn question, which the Constitution wisely confides to the legislative department of the government.[6]

It is clear that Madison was of the firm conviction that the issue of war or peace was a question for the representatives of the people in Congress to decide. In 1812 Congress decided to go to war by a vote of 19 to 13 in the Senate and 79 to 49 in the House. Over 30 years after James Madison's message to Congress, James Polk took a different view of the proper role of the President.

Polk View

President James K. Polk was determined to acquire Texas and California for the expansion of southern slavery and to fulfill a national "manifest destiny." He had determined that a war with Mexico would be necessary to acquire these lands and that the government in Mexico City should be made to appear the aggressor.[7] He thus ordered an American cavalry unit into an area of disputed land between the recently established Republic of Texas and the Rio Grande. One year later, in April, 1846, Mexico attacked American forces and on May 11 Polk requested a declaration of war from the Congress. The House acted with "dispatch" and approved a declaration of war resolution within hours; the Senate complied with Polk's request the next day. War had been made inevitable by the President's conduct of foreign affairs; in the end Congress appeared to have no choice between war and peace.

Lyndon Johnson View

President Johnson presented Congress with a similar *fait accompli* in the early stages of the Vietnam War. On orders of the President, the destroyers *Maddox* and *Turner Joy* were sent on a sensitive mission off the North Vietnamese coast. On August 4, 1964, an alleged North Vietnamese attack on these U.S. vessels occurred in the Gulf of Tonkin; President Johnson sought and received a resolution from the Congress which he regarded as open-ended authority to pursue the war in Southeast Asia in any manner he thought proper. According to Robert Sherrill, a *New York Times* interpretation of the Department of Defense study the so-called Pentagon Papers, indicates that Congress was asked to endorse an action which was an outgrowth of the President's actions for the preceding six months:

> . . . for six months before the Tonkin Gulf incident in August, 1964, the United States had been mounting clandestine military attacks against North Vietnam while planning to obtain a Congressional resolution that the Administration regarded as the equivalent of a declaration of war.[8]

Congress often becomes a party to the President's expansion of his war-making powers because the lawmakers rely upon the executive for their source of information. Senator Case's bill, which became law in 1972, has opened up the door to a congressional demand for information from the executive branch on all future executive agreements. In 1972 the Senate Foreign Relations Committee endorsed another measure (S2224) to require the Central Intelligence Agency (CIA) to provide Congress with certain intelligence information so that it can make more informed policy decisions. However, the Senate has taken no further action on the proposal.

Presidential Interventionism

On what legal basis have Presidents expanded their power to initiate and wage war? Four major developments have led to the expansion of power by the executive and the corresponding decline in congressional control.

First, the President can use the nineteenth-century "neutrality theory" to protect American life and property abroad. This vague prerogative was used as justification for Eisenhower's dispatch of U.S. Marines to Lebanon in 1958, for Lyndon Johnson's use of troops in the Dominican Republic in 1965, and for Richard Nixon's invasion of Cambodia in April, 1970, as well as for U.S. support for the South Vietnamese invasion of Laos in February, 1971. As President Johnson said in 1965, "99 percent of our reason for going in there was to try to provide protection for American lives." [9]

The second legal basis is to repel a "sudden attack" on the United States, which includes our armed forces and bases throughout the world. President Truman used this to justify the American-United Nation's intervention in South Korea; Lyndon Johnson used the same justification for the early bombing of North Vietnam. Presidential action as commander-in-chief can trigger a chain of events in which U.S. forces operating in a sensitive area are attacked. Polk's dispatching of troops along the Rio Grande in 1845 provoked the Mexican army to attack American forces. Similarly, the presence of the destroyers *Maddox* and *Truner Joy* off the North Vietnamese coast on a "snooping mission" led to the "incident" which precipitated the large-scale American involvement in Southeast Asia. The defensive war doctrine was first used by Alexander Hamilton in 1801 when he criticized President Jefferson for his slowness in responding to the attacks by the Barbary pirates. Hamilton's view was that the Constitution intended "that it is the peculiar and exclusive province of Congress, when the nation is at peace, to change that state into a state of war," but "when a foreign nation declares or openly and avowedly makes war upon the United States, they are then by the very fact already at war and any declaration on the part of Congress is nugatory; it is at least unnecessary." [10]

A third rationale for American involvement is collective "security obligations" to which we have become committed since World War II. This "pactomania" has committed us to the defense of 43 nations since World War II. For example, the war in South Vietnam was expanded and U.S. troops sent to that country under the pretext of our participation in the SEATO (Southeast Asian Treaty Organization) pact. Interestingly, Britain and France, also signatories to this security treaty, did not feel obligated to send troops to the defense of South Vietnam.

Fourth, the shift in war making from Congress to the President has resulted from the extension of the "war period." As early as 1939, President Roosevelt proclaimed a "limited national emergency," and in the summer of 1941 he ordered American war vessels to sink enemy ships in our defensive waters. Vast emergency economic powers were extended to President Roosevelt for waging total war. A state of war with Japan existed until President Truman signed a document terminating this condition on April 28, 1952.[11] The expansion of emergency powers during war periods has been so extensive—and so often accompanied by congressional cooperation—that we must now examine the various kinds and uses of these emergency powers.

National Emergencies

International crises and emergencies have added greatly to presidential war-making power. While Congress was in adjournment during the opening days of the Civil War, Lincoln increased the size of the army and navy and called for 80,000 volunteers as well as ordering the purchase of 19 naval vessels. In the early months of the war he ordered the naval blockade of southern ports. The Congress and the Supreme Court supported these actions after the fact.[12]

With the advent of the "total war" concept of World Wars I and II, the President's powers mushroomed. In the first week of World War I President Wilson, acting under his authority as commander-in-chief, created a Committee on Public Information to institute a system of "voluntary" news censorship. By executive order Wilson created the War Industries Board to exert wide-ranging control over industry, including the power to withhold fuel and transportation if the industries did not comply with its requests. Recalcitrant firms faced the prospect of government take-over. Rexford G. Tugwell calls Wilson's economic controls "the most fantastic expansion of the Executive known to the American Experience."[13] Among other things Congress authorized the President to requisition food, fuel, and other supplies necessary for any public use connected with national defense; to take over and operate the railroads; and to regulate the importation, manufacture, storage, mining, and distribution of any necessities.

No less dramatic were Franklin D. Roosevelt's emergency actions during World War II. In 1940 he gave 50 reconditioned destroyers to Britain in exchange for 99-year leases of British naval bases in the Caribbean. In 1941, before Pearl Harbor, he ordered American troops to occupy Greenland and Iceland. These acts were justified by President Roosevelt under his power as commander-in-chief. By executive order he created 29 war agencies under the Office of Emergency Management, directly responsible to the President. Within hours after the Japanese attack on Pearl Harbor, he created military war zones in the United States and detained 70,000 American citizens of Japanese ancestry in "relocation camps" for much of the war. Congress approved this action and the Supreme Court supported this exercise of emergency power in *Korematsu* v. *United States* (1944).[14] Total war had clearly brought about the need for the exercise of total power. There are presently some 470 laws delegating emergency power to the President, ranging from suspending the writ of habeas corpus to placing the entire nation under martial law. These laws are presently being reviewed by the Senate Special Committee on Termination of the National Emergency, chaired jointly by Senators Frank Church (D.-Ida.) and Charles Mathias (R.-Md.). Recommendation for repeal of some of this legislation can be expected now that Congress has concluded its investigation of impeachment charges against President Nixon.[15] In the meantime, the United States has lived under a state of national emergency, never rescinded, since Roosevelt's proclamation of March 5, 1933.[16]

Presidential Advantages: Real or Imagined?

Exponents of presidential authority claim that the area of foreign affairs is so complex and fluid that it is best left under the leadership of the executive. These advocates of presidential power insist that only the executive branch possesses the *unity, expertise, secrecy,* and *speed* necessary to respond to the continual changes in today's world. Several presidential scholars have questioned the wisdom of congressional incursions into the realm of foreign affairs. Concluding that aggressive action by the executive has resulted from legislative incompetence, James MacGregor Burns states that "Obviously the President and Congress cannot be equal partners in war. The legislative branch lacks the single-mindedness, the dispatch, and the information that are essential." [17] Let's reexamine the qualities claimed for presidential leadership to ascertain their validity in practice.

Singleness of leadership and "unity" in policy making are said to be attributes of the executive branch. The President contols a vast number of agencies having overlapping jurisdiction and functions. Seeing this as a problem in foreign affairs, the Congress created the National Security Council (NSC) in 1947 to coordinate foreign policy. However, the bargaining and vote-trading which is endemic in Congress has occurred in the National Security Council as well. Samuel Huntington, 13 years after the creation of the NSC, concluded that "Just as Congress often wrote tariff legislation by giving each industry the protection it wanted, the NSC and the Joint Chiefs make decisions on weapons by giving each service what it desires." [18] Clearly, it is not unusual for the left hand not to know what the right hand is doing in the far-flung federal bureaucracy. Finally, one can note that the President's real power is his power to persuade others to do what he would like them to do.

The President does not sit in the Oval Office and command bureaucrats under him to follow orders. Richard Neustadt quotes a frustrated Franklin D. Roosevelt discussing the lack of ability to command:

> The Treasury is so large and far-flung and ingrained in its practices that I find it is almost impossible to get the action and results I want—even with Henry [Morgenthau] there. But the Treasury is not to be compared with the State Department. You should go through the experience of trying to get any changes in the thinking, policy, and action of the career diplomats and then you'd know what a real problem was. But the Treasury

and the State Department put together are nothing compared with the Na-a-vy. The admirals are really something to cope with—and I should know. To change anything in the Na-a-vy is like punching a feather bed. You punch it with your right and you punch it with your left until you are finally exhausted, and then you find the damn bed just as it was before you started punching.[19]

Another quality claimed for executive leadership in foreign affairs is its ability to draw upon the fact-gathering services of the departments and agencies, such as the State Department, Central Intelligence Agency (CIA), and the Bureau of Foreign and Domestic Commerce. John Kennedy became disenchanted with expert advice early in his administration when the CIA "experts" advised him that there would be a popular uprising in Castro's Cuba following a landing of exiled troops at the Bay of Pigs. Kennedy reported that "I didn't have trustworthy information or I wouldn't have gone on with it." [20] When Lyndon Johnson saw the "light at the end of the tunnel" between 1965 and 1968 in Vietnam, he apparently did not have reliable information. "Selective perception" by the expert in assessing the large quantities of information available has led to mismanagement in arms procurement such as the C-5A jet transport cost overrun of $2 billion. Many errors of "expert judgment" are classified as secret. The testimony by A. E. Fitzgerald, former Deputy for Management Systems for the Air Force, cost him his civil service job for exposing the cost overrun on the C-5A before a congressional committee.[21] It can be argued that debate in congressional committees may eliminate the chances of "selective perception" on the part of bureaucratic experts. If the information is classified as secret, committee members should be examined for clearance and be given an opportunity to review the information and make recommendations to the President.

Some presidential defenders argue that speed is vitally important in responding to fast-moving events in foreign affairs. It is clear that in crisis situations where Presidents must decide quickly on commitment of American armed forces, the ability to act swiftly is crucial. Such action and the information for such a decision should be made available subsequently to Congress for its review and appraisal. In the nonemergency areas of foreign affairs where military commitment is not essential, the Congress should play an active role of advise and consent. For example, whether the U.S. should commit itself to the aid and defense of the white racist minority government in South Africa against the black liberationists is a question which should involve the people's representatives in Congress.

There is even a question of how swiftly the President is able to act in foreign affairs. During the Cuban missile crisis John F. Kennedy was told, much to his dismay, that Khrushchev was demanding the removal of obsolete Jupiter missiles from Turkey in exchange for the withdrawal of Soviet missiles from Cuba. Kennedy had ordered their removal from Turkish soil months earlier. In another incident President Kennedy ordered a change in attitude by our embassy officials in Rome toward the Nenni Socialists.[22] This change occurred only after continuous prodding by the White House.

Congressional Actions to Curb War-Making Power

Three congressional measures passed in 1972 and 1973 have increased the ability of the Congress to curb executive prerogatives in the field of foreign affairs when exercised against the will of Congress. The Case bill, which became law in 1972, requires the executive to transmit executive agreements to the Congress within 60 days of their execution. The other two measures were outgrowths of slowly building congressional and public opposition to the controversial Vietnam War—a conflict fought without a formal declaration of war. In late June, 1973, Congress, for the first time, voted to cut off funds during a military operation when it voted to cut off funds for bombing in Cambodia after August 15, 1973. President Nixon accepted this curtailment of his power only after it was clear that Congress would override any presidential veto. Congress did just that in one of the most far-reaching acts ever passed to restrict the President's use of military forces in foreign combat—the War Powers Act of 1973. Congress recognized that it must give the President the authority to act swiftly in emergencies, but it warned future Presidents that the lawmakers will scrutinize these acts more closely before blankchecks will be given to the President. Passed over a presidential veto on November 7, the War Powers Act of 1973 requires the President to report in writing to Congress within 48 hours after he has committed the armed forces to foreign combat. The combat action must end within 60 days unless Congress authorizes the commitment, but it can be extended for 30 days if the President certifies that this is necessary for a safe withdrawal of forces. Within that 60- or 90-day period Congress can order an immediate removal of U.S. military forces by adopting a concurrent resolution which is not subject to a presidential veto.[23]

Will the congressional actions of the early 70's prove to be merely parchment barriers to the shift of power to the President in foreign military affairs? The repeal of the Gulf of Tonkin Resolution in 1969, the Executive Agreements Act of 1972, the cut-off of appropriations for the bombing of Cambodia, and the War Powers Act of 1973 are all attempts to reassert a proper role for Congress. Perhaps more importantly, congressmen have begun to recognize the importance of creating a state of mind in the executive branch which is not one of arrogance and thoughtlessness in foreign military adventures. This attitude will be created and continued only if Congress keeps a vigil over unilateral executive commitments in foreign military actions.

It is not enough to say that Congress should play a role in shaping the broad contours of American foreign policy if it continues to leave the day-to-day operations in this area to the executive. This policy can easily lead to "commitment by accretion." Congress must develop the mechanisms and the will to participate in setting policies and monitoring these policies and operations on a regular basis.

Congress can rely upon its power of the purse to control the executive branch, but as John Stennis stated in 1972, "cutting off the money after we are in combat is very drastic—I'd hate to see the precedent set." But he added, "It's [constitutionally] possible to cut off appropriations once they're made." [24] Congress withdrew its authorization for the Gulf of Tonkin Resolution in 1969. Seeing no response from the executive it finally decided to cut off funds after August 15, 1973. This ended American military involvement in Indochina.

Unfinished Business

Congress has done much in recent years to curtail specific areas of presidential abuse of power. If passed by Congress, the Ervin bill would ensure that executive agreements on which a majority of both houses were not in accord could be vetoed within 60 days. In addition, the Case bill to require the President to submit military commitments in executive agreements to the Senate as treaties is another measure that would prevent the commitment by accretion which has occurred too often in the past.

Saul Padover has suggested that ceilings be established by Congress on the number of U.S. forces stationed overseas when the nation is not in a state of war.[25] The President would be forced to come to the Congress when these limits were exceeded in a certain region of the world. This suggestion should be considered by Congress, but enough flexibility should be left to the President so that he is not forced to conduct foreign policy in a straitjacket but rather within the limits of proper consultation. President Truman was not hampered when Congress, after the "Great Debate" in 1951, established maximum troop levels in Europe and resolved that the executive should seek congressional approval before sending additional troops. Through its foreign affairs committees, Congress could reexamine the doctrines of American foreign policy espoused by past American Presidents and develop overall policy objectives with the executive branch. Finally, the secretary of state should be present when major policy doctrines are debated on the floor of the House and the Senate.

Public Support of Presidents during Wartime

Public support for the President nearly always increases immediately following decisive presidential action in foreign affairs. This was true during the American involvement in the Bay of Pigs invasion as well as the Cuban missile crisis. The support given presidential action in foreign affairs is illustrated when we compare the polls taken before the American bombing of Hanoi and Haiphong in 1965–66 with those taken after the bombing had begun.

Table 5.1 shows how public opinion shifted from majority oppostion prior to the bombing to 85 percent support of the Johnson Administration after the bombing had begun.

TABLE 5.1 **Public Attitude Toward U.S. Bombing of North Vietnam**

BEFORE BOMBING	Favor Bombing	Oppose Bombing	Total * Percent
Do you think the administration is wrong in not bombing Hanoi or Haiphong?			
September, 1965	30	70	100
February, 1966	42	58	100
May, 1966	50	50	100
BOMBING BEGUN			
Do you think the administration is more right or more wrong in bombing Hanoi and Haiphong?			
July, 1966	85	15	100

*Those with no opinion omitted.

Source: Harris poll, June 13, 1966 as quoted in John E. Mueller *War, Presidents and Public Opinion* (New York: John Wiley & Sons, Inc., 1973), p. 70.

Public support of a President is again shown by the fact that, from 1950 to 1970 a majority of Americans had consistently opposed the admission of Communist China to the United Nations. After President Nixon announced plans to visit China, a majority of those expressing an opinion favored the admission of Communist China.[26]

With this in mind it is noteworthy that in a Gallup poll conducted during the week preceding the congressional override of President Nixon's veto of the War Powers Act, 80 percent of the respondents said that the President should be required to get congressional approval before sending armed forces into foreign action. The Gallup release stated that 58 percent of those questioned said that Congress should not be required "to obtain the approval of the people by means of a national vote" in order to declare war.[27] Clearly, the public feels that the President should not commit this nation's armed forces without the expressed approval of Congress.

PRESIDENT AND CONGRESS: WHO CONTROLS THE DIRECTION OF DOMESTIC POLICY?

The President's role as chief legislator is one of the most visible and publicized functions of his office. A "batting average" of the President's success with his legislative proposals is regularly computed and analyzed in the press. Executive vetoes receive front-page headlines and an overridden veto seems to call for extensive analysis by journalists to determine whether or not the President has lost his leverage with Congress. The formal legislative powers conferred upon the President by the Constitution are few compared to the explicit grant of powers to the Congress. But presidential powers have been greatly expanded through custom and tradition.

Legislative Powers

Article I, section 1 of the United States Constitution vests "*all* legislative powers herein granted," in a Congress consisting of a Senate and a House of Representatives. Section 8 of the same article enumerates 18 areas of legislation, the last one being the so-called "elastic clause" which allows Congress to pass all laws "necessary and proper" for carrying into effect the powers granted it by the Constitution. Despite this explicit assignment of legislative powers to the Congress, it is customary to speak of the President as the chief legislator.

Article II, section 3 empowers the President to recommend measures for congressional consideration, call special sessions, and set the time of adjournment in certain circumstances. By using the power to suggest measures for congressional consideration, Presidents have had a ready forum to outline the goals of their administrations. Woodrow Wilson's New Freedom, Franklin D. Roosevelt's New Deal, John Kennedy's New Frontier, Lyndon Johnson's Great Society, and most recently, Richard Nixon's New Federalism were placed before Congress in State of the Union addresses and special messages. These recommendations have served as the agenda for congressional law-making activities. In the modern era, from Franklin D. Roosevelt on, the Congress has performed the function of disposing of presidential suggestions. The power to call special sessions was employed successfully by President Harry S. Truman in 1948 to kick off his reelection campaign. He challenged the Republican-controlled "do-nothing" 80th Congress to enact legislation from its own GOP platform during a special session called after the national conventions. The power to set the time of adjournment when both houses disagree has never been used by the President.

Veto Power

One of the most powerful weapons in the President's legislative arsenal is the veto. Even if a hostile Congress refuses to pass the bills which the chief executive recommends, the President still possesses the authority to block legislation with which he disagrees. Within ten days of passage, he can return a bill to Congress detailing his objections. Unless both houses of Congress can muster a two-thirds majority, the President's veto is sustained.

Over the years the veto has become a powerful weapon in the hands of the chief executive. Relatively few vetoes—approximately 3 percent or 80 of 2314—were overridden between 1789 and 1974 (see Table 6.1). Although primarily a defensive weapon to be employed by a President to block legislative action, the mere threat of the veto is so formidable that most Presidents can win legislative compromise simply by spreading the word on Capitol Hill that they are considering a veto. Repeatedly, the threat of a veto has brought legislation into line with presidential desires.

President Franklin D. Roosevelt's total of 633 vetoes issued

TABLE 6.1 Presidential Vetoes, 1789–1974

	Regular Vetoes	Pocket Vetoes	Total Vetoes	Vetoes Overridden
Washington	2	—	2	—
Madison	5	2	7	—
Monroe	1	—	1	—
Jackson	5	7	12	—
Tyler	6	3	9	1
Polk	2	1	3	—
Pierce	9	—	9	5
Buchanan	4	3	7	—
Lincoln	2	4	6	—
A. Johnson	21	8	29	15
Grant	45	49	94	4
Hayes	12	1	13	1
Arthur	4	6	12	1
Cleveland	304	109	413	2
Harrison	19	25	44	1
Cleveland	43	127	170	5
McKinley	6	36	42	—
T. Roosevelt	42	40	82	1
Taft	30	9	39	1
Wilson	33	11	44	6
Harding	5	1	6	—
Coolidge	20	30	50	4
Hoover	21	16	37	3
F. Roosevelt	372	261	633	9
Truman	180	70	250	12
Eisenhower	73	106	181	1
Kennedy	11	9	21	—
L. Johnson	16	14	30	—
Nixon	25	16	41	5
Ford	12	15	27	3
Total	1330	979	2314	80

Source: Milton C. Cummings, Jr. and David Wise, *Democracy under Pressure* (New York: Harcourt, Brace and Jovanovich, 1971), p. 387. Data collected from Senate Library, Presidential Vetoes (New York: Greenwood Press, Publishers, 1968), p. iv. Originally published by U.S. Government Printing Office. Data for Kennedy and L. Johnson from Congressional Quarterly Almanac, 1963, 1968 (Washington, D.C.: Congressional Quarterly Service, 1963, 1968), p. 23. Data for Nixon and Ford, *Washington Post* January 12, 1975.

between 1933 and 1945 still stands as an all-time record. On more than one occasion FDR was heard to tell his aides, "Give me a bill that I can veto," as an admonition to keep Congress in line on his main legislative goals. President Kennedy brandished the veto 21 times during his brief 1000 days in the White House. President Johnson was also close to the average with 30 vetoes over a five-year period. President Nixon was not far behind with 20 vetoes during his first term—few of which were overridden. Despite his running battle with Congress in 1973 over impoundment of funds, the Watergate affair, and the Cambodian bombing, President Nixon had seven major vetoes sustained. Only his veto of the War Powers Act was overridden. The decline in the use of the veto from FDR to Nixon can be attributed, in large part, to the fact that since the Roosevelt years the agenda for Congress has been determined by the President.

The lack of the item veto—the authority to reject individual sections of a bill—is an important limitation on the President's veto power. Unlike most state governors, who have this power in appropriations bills, the President must accept or reject an entire bill without modification. As a result, Congress sometimes tacks on "riders" (which may be only distantly related to the main subject of the bill) to legislation that the President wants. Unless the chief executive wants "to throw the baby out with the bath water," he must sign the legislation despite his misgivings about what he considers to be obnoxious riders.

Informal Presidential Power

The formal legislative powers of the President reveal little about his real powers in securing passage of "must" legislation. The President does not command senators and congressmen; he attempts to persuade them. In the words of presidential advisor Richard Neustadt:

The essence of a President's persuasive task with Congressmen and everybody else, *is to induce them to believe that what he wants of them is what their own appraisal of their own responsibilities requires them to do in their interest, not his.*[1]

The President's persuasive power is related positively to the state of his "professional reputation" and "public prestige." To maintain his "professional reputation" with congressmen and senators, he must use a carrot-and-stick approach. He can reward those who support him through patronage and by approving congressional "pet projects." He can punish those who oppose his goals by denying these congressmen government contracts in their districts and by limiting their patronage. Through this system of rewards and punishment, he enhances his own power. He must complete this strategy by acting decisively and by maintaining public support for his programs. Without high "public prestige" congressmen and senators will feel freer to defy the wishes of the President.

Personal phone calls to congressmen or invitations to the White House are among the most effective informal pressures used by Presidents. Few are the legislators, especially those of the President's own party, who will turn down the President's personal request for support of White House-backed legislation after a heart-to-heart talk in the Oval Office. The contrasting sales techniques of two recent Presidents have been described as follows:

> Lyndon Johnson was well-known for his aggressive, hard-sell approach. An experienced member of Congress, Johnson brought the tactics of that branch of government to the Presidency. He would wheedle, cajole, and bulldoze his listener until he got the response he was after. Richard Nixon, a lawyer and a veteran of the low-key Eisenhower administration, is more of a soft-sell President. His favorite line is, "I know you have problems with this, and I will completely understand if you can't come with me. But if you can, I'd appreciate it.[2]

The President has additional tools to help achieve his legislative objectives. His appointive power is one of the most useful. Although the President's power of patronage is now limited by civil service regulations, several thousand presidential appointments—most of them high level and well paid—can still be made with the goal of obtaining legislative objectives.

In the final analysis, time and political circumstance, as well as the personal magnetism and persuasiveness of the chief executive determine how much influence a President actually exerts as a legislative leader. President Franklin D. Roosevelt, whose record of legislative accomplishment is still unmatched, found that his ability to lead was affected by the ebb and flow of events. FDR's first administration achieved a legislative record that included passage of the first Social Security program, the Wagner Act on labor relations, the establishment of the Securities and Exchange Commission, the establishment of the Tennessee Valley Authority (TVA), an Agricultural Adjustment Act that established price supports for agricultural commodities, plus a wide variety of anti-depression relief programs. But during his second administration Roosevelt discovered that his ill-fated "court packing" plan, coupled with his attempted "purge" of conservative antiadministration Democrats in the 1938 primary elections severely weakened his influence on Capitol Hill. However, the outbreak of World War II gave Roosevelt decisive influence once again, this time as commander-in-chief. President Lyndon Johnson's legislative record on his Great Society programs during 1965–66 approached FDR's record of accomplishments. However, his dispatch of 500,000 American troops to Vietnam and their inability to defeat the Viet Cong and North Vietnamese cost him dearly in national political influence and trust. By the spring of 1968, his national popularity in the Gallup polls had plummeted to such a low point (35 percent) that he decided against seeking reelection.

Theoretically, the constitutional separation of powers could result in a deadlock if the presidency is in the hands of one party and Congress is controlled by the opposition party. The tenure of office of the President is independent of the will of Congress; Congress cannot force the resignation of an unpopular President, nor can the President dissolve a recalcitrant Congress. This could present both advantages and disadvantages, as the founding father anticipated. The emergence of political parties has helped bridge the gap between the two branches of government, and most Presidents and legislators have recognized that the checks and balances system cannot function without considerable give-and-take between the President and Congress.

President: The Great Initiator

Although technically Congress is *the* legislative branch of government, the President has become, in fact, the chief initiator of legislation. The Budget and Accounting Act of 1921 placed responsibility for preparing an executive budget with the President and provided a Bureau of the Budget in the Department of the Treasury to assist him in preparing the budget for the federal government. By executive order Franklin D. Roosevelt strengthened his control over the Bureau. He moved it into the Executive Office of the President under the authority granted him by the Executive Reorganization Act of 1939.[3] All program proposals from agencies and departments are screened by the Bureau, and proposed legislation from the agencies must receive its stamp of approval before going on to Capitol Hill. Legislative clearance in the Bureau provides the President with an opportunity to compare bureaucratic proposals with his own legislative program. It has recently been estimated that 50 to 80 percent of all legislation enacted by Congress originates in the executive branch and is filtered through the central clearance apparatus.[4] President Nixon took the final step toward centralizing control of departmental programs in March, 1970, when the Bureau of the Budget was reorganized as the Office of Management and Budget (OMB). Henceforth, OMB changed its emphasis to program evaluation, that is, assessing the degree to which programs are achieving their intended results. The former functions of the Bureau were transferred to the President, to be delegated as he saw fit.[5]

Most legislative issues selected for serious attention and consideration in any session of Congress have usually been placed on the agenda by the President. An item which reaches a formal agenda may have been originated by a member of Congress, a congressional committee staff member, those who use the services of an agency, an agency staff report, or a presidential task force. Unquestionably there is much interaction in this process, but most importantly, items are not likely to receive any significant degree of attention in Congress unless they have been included in one of the many agenda-setting messages presented to the Congress by the President.[6] Remarks by the Chairman of the House Foreign Affairs Committee to an administration witness in 1953 are instructive on how the process works: "Don't expect us to start from scratch on what you people want. That's not the way we do things here—*you* draft the bills and *we* work them over." [7]

Presidential Messages

One of the trump cards the President holds in dealing with Congress is the presidential message. Since Woodrow Wilson's time, each President has personally delivered his State of the Union message, outlining his views on major legislative proposals. In addition, Franklin D. Roosevelt legitimized the practice of sending bills from the White House to Capitol Hill as administration-supported legislation. Now televised during prime evening hours, the President's message receives top billing throughout the land. Early in the regular congressional session the President submits a budget for the next fiscal year, and from time to time he will also prod Congress with special messages on pending legislation.

President Nixon delivered his 1974 State of the Union message on January 30, 1974, before a live television audience of more than 50 million viewers, emphasizing the success of his administration to date. The President proceeded to set forth major areas in which legislation should be forthcoming, such as increasing revenue sharing, comprehensive health insurance for all Americans, funds for research into the nation's energy needs, reform of our system of federal aid to education, defining and protecting the citizen's right to privacy, welfare reform, and lower tariffs and freer trade among nations. His 3500-word State of the Union address was accompanied by a 20,000-word written message which specified his encyclopedic recommendations for legisla-

Credit: The House Banking and Currency Committee

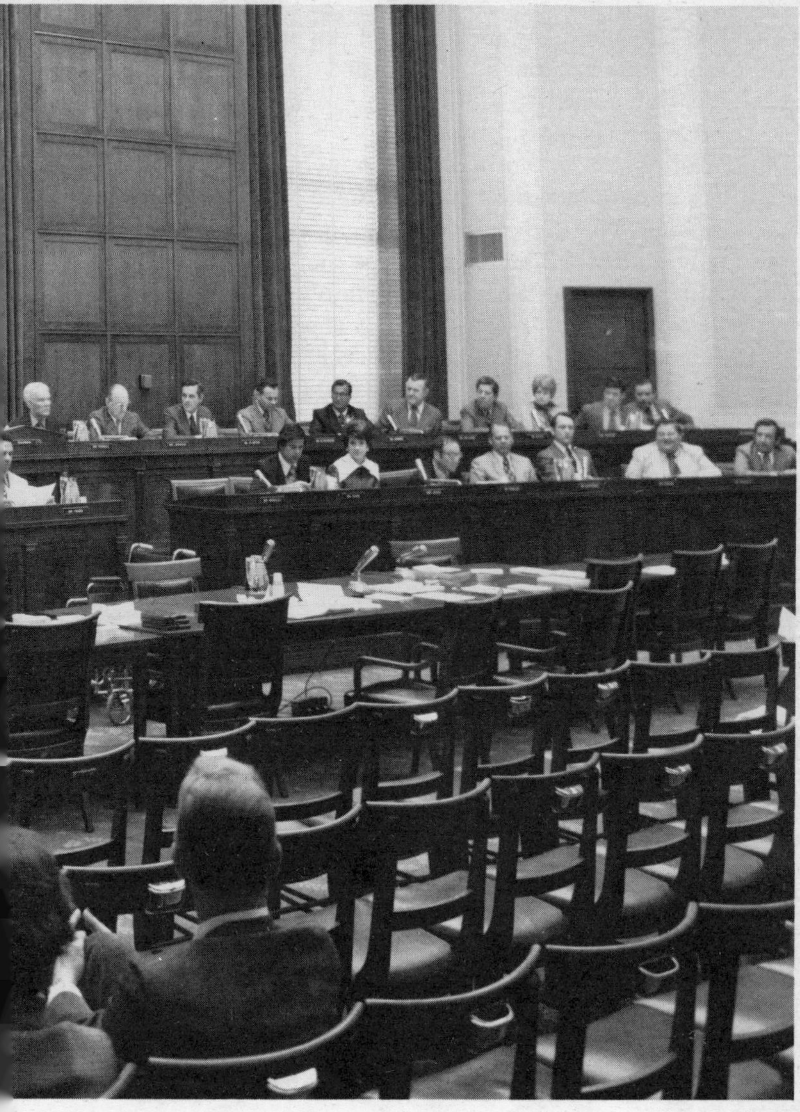

tive action. He closed his address with the comment that "One year of Watergate is enough." This called the nation's attention to his belief that excessive concentration on the Watergate affair might endanger his legislative goals.

The State of the Union address is only one of three major messages communicated to Congress during the opening weeks of each session. The Budget message gives the President an opportunity to outline in monetary terms the policy objectives of his administration. The message describes items of expenditure such as salaries and equipment as well as policies such as revenue sharing, aid to the unemployed, preventing war, and providing low-income housing.[8] In the Economic Report the President lays before Congress recommendations to curb inflation and achieve maximum employment.

Special messages are regularly submitted to the Congress to deal with crises or areas of the President's program that he wishes to emphasize. During his first 100 days as President, Richard Nixon transmitted 14 special messages to the Congress and throughout his two terms he continued to make frequent use of this device. In September, 1973, he took the unusual step of forwarding to Congress a 1500-word State of the Union message which attempted to set a conciliatory tone with an aroused Congress by concluding that "There can be no monopoly of wisdom on either end of Pennsylvania Avenue and there shall be no monopoly of power."[9] Nixon preceded his 1974 State of the Union address with special messages on education, veterans, and energy. In this address he promised that he would also send special messages to Congress on his proposed comprehensive health insurance plan as well as on campaign reform. These were among a barrage of items on which he wished congressional action.

White House Lobbying on Capitol Hill

Presidents often try to anticipate the reaction of congressmen when proposing legislation. President John F. Kennedy delayed sending civil rights legislation to Congress for more than two years for fear that he would alienate southern Democrats whose support he needed on other New Frontier legislative proposals. One scholar of presidential-congressional relations argues that the "law of anticipated reactions" prevents Presidents from sending many proposals to Congress. He concludes: "Much of what we hear about the so-called decline or eclipse or fall of Congress becomes less convincing when we take into account the matters in which Congress always gets its way because the Executive, much as it would like to do such and such, is not sufficiently romantic even to attempt it." [10] Because of the need to anticipate the limits of possible legislation, Presidents employ special assistants who communicate regularly with congressional leaders. Moreover, the need to keep the President's legislative proposals moving through congressional channels has led to a formalization of lobbying for presidential programs.

Woodrow Wilson, the first President to be an active lobbyist on Capitol Hill, was regularly found in the President's room near the senate chamber discussing legislative matters with members of Congress. Franklin D. Roosevelt often dispatched aides such as Tom Corcoran and James Rowe to lobby for his New Deal programs. General Wilton B. Persons, an Eisenhower aide, was the first White House assistant formally assigned to Capitol Hill. Bryce N. Harlow was Eisenhower's liaison contact with the House while Jack Martin concentrated on the Senate. The creation of the Office of Congressional Relations under the direction of Persons marked the institutionalization of White House lobbying activities.

Lawrence (Larry) F. O'Brien was Special Assistant to the President for Congressional Affairs under John Kennedy and Lyndon Johnson from 1961 until late 1965. He perfected the "bridge-building activities" first formalized by Persons. O'Brien and his staff spent half of their time prowling the corridors of the Capitol. O'Brien centralized the liaison activities of the agencies and departments. He required them to give Monday morning reports of the previous week's legislative lobbying and to make projections on the forthcoming week's activities. O'Brien's staff analyzed and condensed these reports on Monday afternoons and presented them to the President for his review on Monday evenings. These reports provided agenda items for the Tuesday morning meetings between congressional leaders and the President. Approximately 40 Congressional Relations staff members assigned to various departments became the congressional foot soldiers in O'Brien's command structure. These agency and department liaison officers were often used to lobby for the President's program among pressure groups and in Congress. Thus, businessmen were contacted by the Department of Commerce and unions by the Department of Labor and urged to support presidential proposals before congressional committees.[11]

Bryce Harlow, formerly an Eisenhower liaison aide, was in charge of President Nixon's Congressional Relations staff. Although he resigned early in the President's second term, he was lured back by Mr. Nixon in October, 1973, to help restore congressional confidence in his "Watergate-tainted" presidency.

President Nixon, in an act of desperation to stop the impeachment proceeding of 1974, personally took command of the White House lobbying effort against impeachment. This presidential strategy included television appearances, travels throughout the country and abroad, and White House dinners as well as evening cruises aboard the presidential yacht, *Sequoia,* intended to persuade doubtful congressmen and senators of the President's innocence.

Reaction to White House lobbying is mixed. Larry O'Brien defends liaison activity, stating, "It is feasible and proper to have a close rapport with the Legislative Branch of Government. . . . After all, we recognize that the President proposes, and it is up to the Legislative Branch of the Government to dispose. But certainly there is no known barrier to constantly advocating our program . . . to the people and to the Congress." [12] The contrasting view is expressed by Representative Thomas B. Curtis (R.-Mo.) who states:

> The Executive Branch of the Federal Government should be forbidden to lobby. They have a forum to be heard in the congressional committees, and they should use it. They also have

the ability to communicate directly with the people, as the President does on TV time, and so forth.

So let's have a cessation of this business of the Executive officials, Cabinet officers, coming into Congressmen's offices. They don't even come before the committees, they come to visit you in your office to sell you on this particular point of view. And I say if you want to say this, say it out in public where the [other] side can hear you, don't come in and talk to me privately unless there is a basic reason.[13]

The centralization of executive lobbying has added to presidential access and influence in the Congress. But congressional resentment of arm-twisting and behind-the-scenes influence by the White House liaison staff will continue to be a source of displeasure to congressmen who feel that this gives additional advantages to an already over-powerful executive branch.

Congressional Legislative Machinery

The rules and procedures of the Congress make it possible for 435 representatives and 100 senators to arrive at collective decisions. The most crucial part of the legislative machinery is the committee system. Over 10,000 bills are introduced each year; of these about 1000 become law. Most of the remaining bills are buried in the committee system. After a bill is introduced in the Senate or the House (all revenue bills must be introduced in the House) it is assigned to one of the 17 standing committees of the Senate or one of the 21 standing committees of the House.[14]

Committee chairmen are the key power figures in committees. They assign bills to subcommittees and schedule hearings of the full committee. Chairmen are selected on the basis of seniority. Thus, the member of the majority party with the longest continuous service on the committee becomes the chairman. In 1971 Republicans in the House initiated a procedure to select ranking committee members by a vote of their caucus. This proposal has been adopted by Republicans in the Senate and Democrats in the House to hold chairmen and ranking minority leaders more accountable. It should be noted, however, that the caucus has continued to apply the rule of seniority.[15]

Stumbling blocks exist throughout the legislative process for legislation unwanted by members of each house. After hearings are held on a bill, the committee either (1) recommends it for adoption, (2) rewrites the bill into a new proposal, (3) kills it by majority vote, or (4) ignores the bill and prevents its passage. In the House, the Rules Committee must assign procedures for the handling of a bill on the floor before it can be considered by the entire House. Appropriations and revenue measures are treated as "privileged motions" and considered without a "rule" attached from the Rules Committee. In the Senate the filibuster allows members to talk an unwanted bill to death. Though it occurs infrequently, a filibuster can be stopped by a two-thirds vote of the senators present. After a bill makes it over these hurdles, it must often face the problem of bicameralism.[16] Each house's version of the bill goes to the House-Senate conference committee, where it is either put into final form through bargaining and compromise or it is killed.

Three major problems confront Congress in dealing with the executive branch: access to independent sources of information, a mechanism for Congress to play a role in setting national priorities, and control over the budgetary process. Congressional committees depend upon information from the agencies which propose the legislation in the first place. Agency selectivity in providing information is sometimes obstructed by committee staff work or the work of the Congressional Research Service (formerly the Legislative Reference Service) available to members of Congress.

The lack of a congressional mechanism to set priorities for legislation is another major problem. National priorities are now set outside the legislative branch in the Oval Office and in the Office of Management and Budget. Although the Senate approved the Full Opportunity and National Goals and Priorities Act in 1970 and 1972, proponents failed to muster the support necessary for passage in the House. This measure is designed to improve the quantity and quality of information available to Congress. It would create an Office of Goals and Priorities Analysis within the legislative branch which would "conduct a continuing analysis of national goals and priorities [to] . . . provide the Congress with information, data, and analysis necessary for enlightened priority decisions." [17]

The Budget and Accounting Act of 1921 gives the President the responsibility for preparing an executive budget to be submitted to Congress during January of each calendar year. Congress then turns this budget package over to its revenue committees in the House (Ways and Means) and the Senate (Finance) and to its appropriations committees, where it is divided up so that the appropriations subcommittees can consider the various sections. At present, however, appropriations bills are considered independently of one another and of the amount of money available to finance them. Thus, until the end of the calendar year, no one in Congress or elsewhere in the federal government knows how much spending will be authorized or how large the surplus or deficit will be. As a result of these antiquated budgetary procedures, over the years Congress has yielded real control over most budget decisions to the White House. Up to this time, only the President, who has a well-staffed, centralized Office of Management and Budget consisting of approximately 500 fiscal experts, has been capable of coordinating all parts of the budget into an integrated whole.

By the spring of 1974, however, Congress finally decided to reclaim the budgetary decision-making powers that had passed to the White House through congressional sloth and disorganization. Intent on recapturing the constitutional power of the purse from the White House, the Senate voted 80 to 0 in late March, 1974, to approve a revolutionary congressional procedure for handling the government's $300 billion annual budget. The new bill, which was agreed upon by a House-Senate conference committee on June 5, 1974, and approved by both houses of Congress on June 22, 1974, will lead to a wholesale overhauling of congressional budget procedures and the setting of national spending priorities. Although the White House played little part in the formulation of the measure, Mr. Nixon signed the final version into law on July 12, 1974.[18]

The radical new provisions of the Congressional Budget and

Impoundment Control Act of 1974 create budget committees in both houses to consider all federal spending each year as a package, to fix a target surplus or deficit, to clamp a ceiling on total outlays and to divide the total among 14 broad categories, such as education and defense, and thus assign spending priorities. If the federal expenditure and revenue figures do not equal the amount of spending and revenue ordered by the various spending and taxation bills, both houses will pass a reconciliation bill. This bill will mandate cuts or additions to any or all of the appropriations or tax bills so that the budget deficit or surplus will be identical with the figure set down in a final concurrent resolution passed by both houses. In such cases, neither house of Congress will adjourn until the reconciliation bill has become law.

Equally important, the new legislation creates a Congressional Office of the Budget to furnish technical expertise to the lawmakers. Until now Congress has had to rely largely upon White House spokesmen for information on how to slice the budget pie and also for technical data—frequently presented to support the President's view on spending priorities. Thus, under the new law, Congress will for the first time be equipped to make sound budget decisions.

Sponsors of the budget reform legislation (as well as other budget experts) have long pointed out that the major problem in congressional budget making is that each of the 14 or 15 appropriations bills is handled separately without any computation of the total amount of spending. Furthermore, there are "back door spending" bills that do not go through the appropriations process but simply authorize various agencies to obtain money directly from the Treasury.

This new legislation also sharply limits the President's authority to impound or refuse to spend money appropriated by Congress and forbids him to impound funds as a tool of fiscal policy—a provision that Mr. Nixon may have swallowed with considerable difficulty.

Under the Congressional Budget and Impoundment Control Act of 1974, the start of the federal government's fiscal year, previously July 1, has been changed to October 1. The July starting date often found half of the government agencies unfunded. In the period from 1964 to 1974 only six money bills were passed before the July 1 deadline. Consequently, Congress often had to pass temporary funding measures to keep programs going.

After the unanimous senate vote on the budget reform bill, Senator Sam Ervin (D.-N.C.), a sponsor of the bill who has served in the Senate for 20 years, observed, "This measure is one of the most important pieces of legislation considered during my service in the Senate, and I do not say that lightly . . . a Congress that cannot control spending cannot effectively control the executive branch either." [19]

Although the Congressional Budget and Impoundment Control Act of 1974 is no cure-all for the ills of Congress, it will better enable Congress to carry out the intent of the Constitution to give to Congress the power of the purse. Not since the early years of the Republic (when the House of Representatives considered the budget under the "committee of the whole" procedure and the Ways and Means Committee filled in the details) has the Congress been able to fully control the federal purse. Over the years the two houses of Congress have fragmented appropriations bills into committees which take little consideration of the budget as a whole. The new measure provides the mechanism for Congress to reassert its control both over domestic spending priorities and the far-flung programs of the federal government.

Congressional Delegation of Power

Presidential authority has increased in part through congressional delegation of legislative powers. By means of this practice, Congress enacts broad, general legislation and allows the President to "fill in the details"—a procedure that has developed from a practical need. Because Congress cannot anticipate all the consequences of its legislation in such complex fields as, for example, labor relations or environmental protection, Congress may limit itself to, sketching the broad outlines of policy and authorize those in the executive branch who have administrative expertise to fill in the specifics.

The authority of the executive branch to fill in the details of legislation falls under the President's consititutional power to see that the laws are "faithfully executed." The President often subdelegates to executive officials in the federal agencies the authority to establish rules and regulations to interpret statutes. In the period from 1936 to 1970, the time period during which the rules and regulations of the executive branch have been published in the *Code of Federal Regulations,* more than 100 volumes have been published citing thousands of rules which interpret statutes.[20]

In addition, Presidents issue executive orders which have the force of law when they are founded upon either constitutional powers or statutory authority. Since 1907 executive orders have been numbered; by August 15, 1971, there were 11,615 and estimates of as many as 50,000 unnumbered orders.[21] Executive orders have been interpreted by the Supreme Court as having the force of laws passed by the Congress.

The best-known recent example of this type of "blank-check" legislation was the congressional action of 1970 which granted standby power to the President to impose price and wage controls for one year in the event of a national economic emergency. Faced with spiraling prices and wages, President Nixon, to the surprise of many Capitol Hill observers, invoked this standby legislation in August, 1971. With renewed authority from Congress each year, President Nixon maintained these ceilings for almost three years, except for five months in early 1973.

In his 1962 legislative program, President John F. Kennedy asked Congress for standby authority to reduce taxes and increase spending as the economic health of the nation required. Under this proposal the President would have had the authority to uniformly reduce all individual tax rates by as much as 5 percent, providing his action was not rejected within 30 days by a joint resolution of the Congress. In addition, if unemployment increased by at least 1 percent during a specified number of months, the President would have had the discretion to accelerate or initiate the spending of up to $2 billion in capital improvement projects. Many members of Congress considered this an executive usurpation of the congressional prerogatives to control taxation and spending. Representative Wilbur Mills (D.-Ark.), Chairman of the House Ways and Means Committee, received the bill but took no further action.[22]

In September, 1972, Richard Nixon sought an unprecedented peacetime delegation of power. He proposed a $250 billion ceiling on the 1973 fiscal budget and requested the Congress to give him the sole authority to cut spending in areas of *his choice* if Congress approved appropriations exceeding this ceiling. This would have been tantamount to an item veto. Historically, Congress had refused to accept suggestions for a constitutional amendment that would have granted the President an item veto similar to that granted to governors in more than 40 states. Although the House voted to support Mr. Nixon's proposal, the Senate refused to accept this presidential request.[23]

Impoundment

President Nixon sought to accomplish his legislative purposes by wholesale impoundment of congressionally appropriated funds. However, Nixon did not invent the impoundment procedure. This device was first used by Thomas Jefferson to defer gunboat construction in 1803. President Truman used it to control spending on a jet-fighter wing he had not requested, and President Kennedy withheld money budgeted for the B-70 bomber in the early 1960's. These impoundment actions were based upon the President's powers as commander-in-chief and on the gounds that such funds could not be allocated economically. President Nixon moved beyond these justifications and refused to spend money which he believed was beyond his own program ceilings. In 1971, he impounded an estimated $12 billion. For example, Congress had authorized and appropriated $18 billion for various domestic programs. Nixon promptly ordered the Office of Management and Budget to spend only $12 billion of this money. The same procedure was followed in such widely divergent programs as interstate highway construction and aid to education.

By early 1973 the political lines had been sharply drawn between congressional leaders and President Nixon. House Speaker Carl Albert declared "The wholesale impoundment of appropriated funds to be the boldest assault on Congress' Constitutional power to govern." [24] In Albert's words, "Impoundments strike at the very heart of Congress' power of the purse, jeopardizing the explicit constitutional right of Congress to appropriate monies." And the Speaker warned, "Take away this power, and Congress is nothing more than a debating society. The votes of the people cast for their representatives would become meaningless acts. Unchecked by this fundamental legislative power, any President would have the autocratic prerogative to do and spend as he pleases." [25] Despite several lower court defeats on impoundment, Roy L. Ash, the President's director of the Office of Management and Budget, declared in mid-September, 1973, "The President is not going to abrogate his responsibility to the people to maintain a non-inflationary budget." [26]

In early October, 1973, President Nixon vetoed a strongly worded antiimpoundment bill. This bill would have required the President to notify Congress of his decisions against spending certain funds. If either house disapproved of his action within 60 days, the funds would be released for spending. Although neither house successfully overrode the President's veto, Mr. Nixon began releasing impounded funds in late 1973 and early 1974. The 1973 congressional uproar over impoundment seems to have been a major factor in restoring the presidential-congressional balance of power that had been tilted in favor of the President for most of the past 75 years.

The Ford Administration, acting under the new impoundment control law for the first time in September, 1974, asked Congress to defer or rescind $20.3 billion in federal budget authority for spending in future years as well as programs dating back a dozen or more years. Mr. Ford requested deferrals of budget authority totaling $19.84 billion in the following major areas: waste treatment construction; federal highway funds; seven programs in the Department of Health, Education, and Welfare; and smaller amounts for programs within the Departments of Agriculture, Commerce, Interior, and State.

Proposed recisions (to terminate spending) totaling near $500 million were requested for only two programs: low-rate Rural Electrification Administration loans and Appalachian Regional Development airport construction.[26]

Congressional Follow-up and Oversight

Congress has developed tools to ensure that its legislative enactments are followed by the executive branch. The Legislative Reorganization Act of 1946 directs each standing committee in the House and Senate to exercise "continuous watchfulness" over administrative agencies and their execution of the law. The act further directs the senate and house Committees on Government Operations to review the economy and efficiency of any executive agency.

Since the passage of the Budget and Accounting Act of 1921, the congressional "watchdog" over executive administration has been the Comptroller General. As the servant of Congress, he is charged with the responsibility of examining federally funded programs for waste and mismanagement. Under the 1970 Legislative Reorganization Act he is directed to make cost-benefit studies of any programs and activities on his own initiative, or when directed by either house of Congress, or by any committee having jurisdiction over federal programs and activities.

As noted earlier in this chapter, Congress lacks adequate information to judge the success of its programs. In 1970 the Congressional Research Service (formerly the Legislative Reference Service) was directed to increase the size of its staff and the scope of its activities to better advise Congress on the operations of executive agencies. However, it is still too early to judge the performance of this staff arm of Congress.

Executive Privilege

The need for congressional information sometimes meets the roadblock of executive privilege when the Congress requests information in areas of "national security," areas that Presidents define as requiring extreme secrecy. It is customary for Presidents to deny the Congress information on communications between himself and his subordinates when this might destroy confidentiality in his administration. President Nixon employed executive privilege on a case-by-case basis. He set down three guidelines for its use on March 11, 1973, reiterating his earlier memorandum circulated in the executive branch on March 24, 1969: (1) All agency and department officials will provide information except when "compelling need" necessitates their receiving approval from the attorney general and the President; (2) cabinet officials will comply with "reasonable" congressional requests for information in all their non-White House capacities; (3) members and former members of the President's White House staff will decline formal requests for appearances before committees except where directed to do so by the President.[27] On May 22, 1973, the President stated that executive privilege would not be invoked as to "testimony concerning possible criminal conduct." The President was by then engulfed in defending his position on the Watergate burglary and cover-up activities of 1972–73.

The limits and legitimacy of the exercise of executive privilege were clarified by the Supreme Court on July 24, 1974, in the landmark cases *United States* v. *Richard M. Nixon* and *Richard M. Nixon* v. *United States*.

In these monumental decisions on subpoenaed presidential tapes and documents, the Supreme Court rejected the White House position based upon a broad interpretation of executive privilege. The White House maintained that only the President could be the final arbiter of when executive privilege could be invoked. Presidential attorney James D. St. Clair argued orally before the Supreme Court that the judiciary should avoid "political questions" and stay its hand in pending criminal cases until impeachment had run its course. He went on to argue that "The President is not above the law," but he added, "We contend that the law applies to him in only one way." [28] That way is through the impeachment process alone.

Special Watergate Prosecutor Leon Jaworski in his oral argument before the Supreme Court, contended that no President has an "absolute right" to refuse to make public confidential conversations. He argued that "this nation's constitutional form of government is in serious jeopardy if the President—any President—is to say that the Constitution means what he says it does, and that there is no one, not even the Supreme Court, to tell him otherwise."[29]

Chief Justice Warren Burger, speaking for a unanimous Supreme Court that included three Nixon appointees, rejected presidential contention of the absolute power of executive privilege by stating:

> When the ground for asserting privilege as to subpoenaed materials sought for use in a criminal trial is based only on the generalized interest in confidentiality, it cannot prevail over the fundamental demands of due process of law in the fair administration of justice. The generalized assertion of privilege must yield to the demonstrated, specific need for evidence in a pending criminal case.[30]

Quoting as precedent Chief Justice John Marshall in the landmark case of *Marbury* v. *Madison* (1803), Chief Justice Burger held that the judiciary must have the final voice to decide the meaning of the law and the Constitution. Marshall ruled that "it is emphatically the province and duty of the Judicial Department to say what the law is."[31] President Nixon, though dismayed by the decision, agreed to abide by the Supreme Court's verdict and hand over the subpoenaed documents as soon as possible.

For the first time in its history, the Supreme Court declared a constitutional basis for the privilege of confidentiality for presidential communications in *U.S.* v. *Nixon*. Chief Justice Burger, again speaking for the Court, held that "Nowhere in the Constitution, as we have noted earlier, is there any explicit reference to a privilege of confidentiality, yet to the extent this interest relates to the effective discharge of a President's powers, it is constitutionally based."[32] In this case the Supreme Court narrowed the application of executive privilege while affirming the constitutional basis for its use.

As noted by presidential attorney James D. St. Clair, only the

House of Representatives can hold the President accountable to the law, through its constitutional power of impeachment. On July 30, 1974, the House Judiciary Committee approved a third article of impeachment citing the President for defying congressional subpoenas and failing to provide information which the Committee felt it needed to investigate charges made against the President. The Committee issued four congressional subpoenas for 62 taped conversations which the President refused to honor. The Judiciary Committee did not challenge the general doctrine of confidentiality and executive privilege, but insisted upon its constitutional power to handle impeachment proceedings.

Appointment and Oversight

Congress has the constitutional power of "pre-oversight" through the role of the Senate in giving advice and consent on appointments. Congress can set forth qualifications for executive officers, and it can determine the number of officers in each agency and their job descriptions.

Though most presidential nominations of prospective cabinet members, federal judges, and ambassadors are approved by the Senate in routine fashion, from time to time the Senate has demonstrated that the President ignores the confirmation process at his own peril. In 1958, for example, the Senate refused to confirm President Eisenhower's nominee for secretary of commerce, Lewis Strauss, by a vote of 46 to 49. Failure to confirm Strauss stemmed from his earlier chairmanship of the Atomic Energy Commission, when he had aroused the ire of Democratic Senator Clinton Anderson of New Mexico, Chairman of the Joint Committee on Atomic Energy. Senator Anderson charged, among other things, that Strauss had not been candid in his relations with the Committee. Strauss had also supported the Eisenhower Administration's opposition to public development and ownership of atomic power installations, much to the chagrin of the Democratic majority in the Senate. The rejection of Strauss was also related to the fact that he had been involved in the Dixon-Yates affair in 1954–55.[33]

More recently, two of President Nixon's first nominees for the U.S. Supreme Court were rejected. Mr. Nixon took the questionable constitutional position that as President he alone had the authority to nominate members of the Supreme Court. In his view, the Senate's duty was merely to confirm his appointments, but he failed to persuade the Senate Democratic majority—and also several senators from his own party. Indeed, the two rejected Supreme Court nominees, Clement Haynsworth of South Carolina and G. Harrold Carswell of Florida, were widely regarded as jurists of limited talents. Haynsworth's nomination also suffered from a charge of conflict of interest, namely, that he had participated in a lower federal court case involving a company in which he held shares of stock. When the next two Supreme Court vacancies occurred, the Senate announced its determination to scrutinize prospective jurists; this action probably helped push Mr. Nixon away from a list of inferior candidates and toward two better qualified men, Justices Lewis Powell and William Rehnquist.

The Senate's recent decision to look more closely at prospective cabinet and other high-level appointees and, if necessary, to hold them as "hostages" for extracting cooperation from President Nixon, contributed to the exposure of additional information in the burgeoning Watergate affair. Early in 1973, Elliot Richardson won senate approval for the attorney generalship only after he pledged to the Senate Judiciary Committee that he would appoint a special prosecutor with complete authority to investigate the Watergate affair. When President Nixon ordered him to violate this pledge and fire Special Prosecutor Archibald E. Cox, Mr. Richardson resigned.

The determination of a few Democratic senators to scrutinize the credentials of L. Patrick Gray, III, as prospective director of the FBI and successor to J. Edgar Hoover, resulted not only in his eventual withdrawal but also in some major breakthroughs in the then embryonic Watergate investigation. Subsequently, the new acting FBI director, William Ruckelshaus (who later became Elliot Richardson's deputy attorney general), played a prominent role in the Watergate investigation. Ruckelshaus ordered the release of the FBI files that disclosed the White House special investigation unit's break-in at Daniel Ellsberg's psychiatrist's office. Ellsberg was under indictment for releasing to the press the so-called Pentagon papers outlining U.S. involvement in the Vietnam War. The acting director of the FBI also announced the discovery of 17 government wiretaps of questionable legality on the telephones of Washington newsmen and several administration (and former) officials.

Another of President Nixon's prospective appointees, Robert H. Morris, a nominee for the Federal Power Commission, was blocked by the Senate in June, 1973. By a vote of 49 to 44, the Senate recommitted Mr. Morris' nomination to the Senate Commerce Committee, ostensibly for further hearings.[34] But Capitol Hill observers readily concluded that Morris' nomination was dead. Senate opponents of Mr. Morris argued that there should be a consumer representative on the Federal Power Commission, which regulates public utilities and the oil and natural gas industries. While senate critics praised Mr. Morris as an able lawyer, they objected to the fact that he had spent 15 years with a law firm that represented one of California's biggest oil companies and had handled matters before the Commission for the company.

Several lawmakers have proposed to check the power of the President by exerting greater control on the White House "palace guard" through the confirmation power. To keep these White House aides more accountable, Senator Walter E. Mondale (D.-Minn.) has urged that all top-level, policy-making presidential aides be subject to confirmation by the Senate.

In early 1973, Congress sought to make the director and deputy director of the Office of Management and Budget—a key agency in the Executive Office of the President—subject to senate confirmation. The Office of Management and Budget exercises comprehensive budgetary and operational control over departments and agencies throughout the federal government. In May, 1973, however, President Nixon vetoed a bill to require confirmation of these two White House officials, and the House of Representatives sustained the veto.

Investigation

One of the most powerful oversight tools that Congress may exercise over a President is the power of investigation. Though one of the most important functions performed by Congress, the investigative power is nowhere mentioned in the Constitution. However, the power of Congress to investigate and gather information may be implied from its broad legislative powers. So important is the function of gathering facts that Woodrow Wilson once wrote that "the informing function of Congress should be preferred even to its legislative functions." [35]

Special investigations of the executive branch have been undertaken since the early days of the Republic. These proceedings are usually started after some dramatic event occurs that demands a public explanation—or perhaps a scapegoat. The first congressional investigation took place in 1793, after General St. Clair's military expedition against the Indians had ended in disaster.

Until the Senate Watergate Committee investigation of the Nixon Administration, the most widely publicized investigation of corruption in the executive branch was the Teapot Dome scandal during the Harding Administration. The chief culprit, Secretary of the Interior Albert Fall, was convicted of accepting a bribe for leasing oil-rich government lands to private speculators. The senate investigation also prompted President Coolidge, who had assumed office after Harding's death in 1923, to begin a thorough housecleaning of the Veteran's Administration and the Justice Department.

Other investigations have uncovered harmful banking, stock exchange, and public utility practices; infringements on civil liberties; and subversive infiltration of government agencies. Not all congressional investigations, however, are aimed at partisan embarrassment of the President and his administration. The Truman Committee, which probed waste and inefficiency during World War II, helped President Roosevelt keep an eye on various defense procurement and production agencies. Indirect recognition for the outstanding work performed by the chairman, Harry

S. Truman (D.-Mo.) came in the form of the Democratic vice-presidential nomination in 1944.

Despite occasional abuses, congressional investigations have performed the valuable role of overseeing the executive branch and checking wrongdoing in high places. Investigations may also be undertaken to influence public opinion. For example, Senator William J. Fulbright (D.-Ark.) tried to demonstrate the folly of American involvement in Vietnam with the Senate Foreign Relations Committee's hearings that began in 1966. Though Senator Fulbright earned the undisguised rancor of President Johnson, his televised hearings contributed to a growing national disillusionment with the continued escalation of American military involvement in Southeast Asia. Clearly, investigations are an important part of our system of checks and balances.

How far may Congress go in investigating the President and the executive branch? More than a decade ago, the U.S. Supreme Court clearly intimated that there is an area of executive privilege into which Congress may not intrude through the use of its investigatory authority. In the words of the Supreme Court:

> Broad as it is the [investigatory] power [of Congress] is not, however, without limitations. Since Congress may only investigate into those areas in which it may potentially legislate or appropriate, it cannot inquire into matters which are within the exclusive domain of one of the other branches of Government. Lacking the judicial power given to the Judiciary, it cannot inquire into matters that are exclusively the concern of the Judiciary. Neither can it supplant the Executive in what exclusively belongs to the Executive.[36]

Until the Watergate affair, presidential refusals to supply information to Congress had usually been accepted in good faith by congressional committees. Indeed, until Watergate Congress had never seen fit to carry its fight to the point of forcing a judicial decision. But the Pandora's box of Watergate scandals opened the door to a series of demands from the Senate Watergate Committee, as well as from the House Judiciary Committee investigating impeachment, for copies of the White House tapes of presidential conversations. As a result, President Nixon retreated several times from his claims of absolute executive privilege.

Before the dust clears from the congressional investigation of the Watergate scandals, the constitutional "twilight zone" separating the working relationships between the President and Congress will probably be further clarified.

Legislative Veto

An interesting oversight device employed by Congress is the legislative veto, where a President is authorized by legislation to put forth executive reorganization plans which automatically become law unless vetoed by Congress. The legislative veto is provided for in statutes which allow the President to reorganize the executive branch. A proposed reorganization may be vetoed by a concurrent resolution passed within 60 days of its submission to the Congress. In March, 1970, President Nixon changed the name of the Bureau of the Budget to the Office of Management and Budget, and reassigned its functions, in part, to the White House itself. This action was not vetoed by the Congress. In addition to a legislative veto by *both houses,* the Congress permits *either house* to veto some measures, such as proposed increases in congressmen's salaries. A third form of the legislative veto is the requirement of the approval of a "specific committee" before a President can take action. President Lyndon Johnson expressed strong opposition to this method, and on one occasion he withheld money from a program set up under a committee-veto provision.[37]

Conclusion

In this chapter we have attempted to present a picture of the role of the President and the Congress in determining the direction of domestic policy. The modern President has become the great initiator and promoter of legislative programs. He makes use of presidential messages, the threat of the veto, his informal powers of persuasion, and White House lobbyists to push his program through the Congress. Congress has become the great disposer of presidential proposals—deciding if they should be enacted, altered, or put on the shelf for possible future consideration. We believe that increasingly a primary function of Congress has become oversight of the executive branch through the control of appointments, the investigation of the President's administration, and the exercise of the veto power where Congress has delegated authority to the President. This new congressional role is illustrated by the recommendation of the Senate Watergate Committee that a special prosecutor, independent of the President, be created to oversee the executive branch. If acted upon by the Congress, this recommendation would demonstrate how investigations by congressional committees ensure executive accountability to the laws of the nation and the Constitution. A second example of this new role of Congress is the veto power established by the War Powers Act of 1973 for long-term foreign military commitment. This act was discussed in Chapter 5.

COOPERATION BETWEEN EXECUTIVE AND LEGISLATIVE BRANCHES

One student of the presidency has observed, "if the Constitution can be said to grant legitimacy to anything, surely it legitimizes conflict between Congress and the President." [1] Indeed, the framers intended that the two coordinate branches should check one another in order to prevent abuses of power. But the founding fathers never intended that Congress and the President should always be at loggerheads. One of our major goals in this chapter is to show that the level and frequency of conflict between the President and Congress has often been overestimated. Several reasons will be given for the usual high degree of cooperation between the Congress and the President, despite the separation of powers doctrine. Later in the chapter we will examine and criticize various proposals that have been advanced to improve presidential-legislative cooperation and suggest some ways to help Congress make the President more accountable than he has been in the past quarter of a century.

Meeting Each Other Halfway

One factor that moderates conflict between the President and Congress is the unofficial moratorium on partisanship that occurs at the start of a President's term of office or when a Vice-President assumes the presidency. This is the so-called "honeymoon" period in which the President is allowed to organize his administration with a minimum of congressional sniping. Even if some senators and congressmen have serious reservations about the President's new appointees, they generally confirm them with minimal scrutiny.

To be sure, the President and Congress frequently have sharp

STATE OF THE UNION. President Truman gives his State of the Union Message to a Joint Session of Congress.

Senate Majority and Minority Leaders   Credit: Mr. Arthur E. Scott

differences over issues or policies, but both sides recognize that for the country to prosper, they must meet each other halfway on many issues. This interplay of sparring, negotiating, and trading off has taken on many aspects of "a ritualized tug-of-war." Yet both the President and Congress know that, as Neustadt has noted, "their powers are so intertwined that neither will accomplish much for very long, without the acquiesence of the other." [2] As a matter of fact, in some matters the Constitution requires joint action by the Senate and the President, for example, the confirmation of high-level presidential appointees and treaty making.

Loose party discipline in Congress, unlike the strict lines of British parliamentary rule, sometimes enables a President to persuade members of the opposition in the House or Senate to cross party lines to support White House-endorsed legislation. For example, President Eisenhower was a master in attracting opposition party support to provide him the margin of victory; he accomplished this 58 times in 1953.[3] More recently, during his first term President Nixon managed to register a number of legislative victories in the areas of defense, foreign policy, and "law and order" by exploiting the split between southern and northern Democrats. Generally, some issues, for example, revenue sharing, water pollution controls, space exploration, and veterans' benefits, enjoy widespread bipartisan support.

The American constitutional system itself encourages a spirit of compromise between the executive and legislative branches. The Congress cannot force the resignation of an uncooperative President, nor can the President dissolve a recalcitrant Congress. Therefore, the two sides usually prefer to find an acceptable compromise rather than remain deadlocked for long periods.

Role of Party

Near the top of the list of factors that facilitate cooperation is the effect of party membership. For persons holding public office and bearing a party label, the party tie is a strong inducement for executive-legislative cooperation. Although major portions of the congressional agenda are determined by the President, the congressional leaders of his party are also anxious to help build a positive legislative record. This observation has been confirmed by students of roll-call voting who have discovered that the best single predictor of a congressman's vote is his party affiliation.[4]

Party ties bridge the gulf between Congress and the White House. Just as some opposition to the President exists within his own party in Congress—over the years, for example, many southern Democrats have voted against the programs of Presidents Roosevelt, Truman, Kennedy, and Johnson—some members of the opposition party regularly support the President's legislative programs. Since the New Deal era, a segment of northern, urban Republicans has frequently backed Democratic presidential programs, especially bills relating to housing, public health, urban rapid transit, education, and civil rights. Cross-party voting coalitions tend to lessen the effects of partisanship and generally decrease conflict within the political system. Bipartisan cooperation in the formulation of some legislation enables both parties to claim credit for programs that are popular or long overdue— for example, the Hill-Burton Act, which aided hospital construction; civil rights legislation, and the 18-year-old vote.

Presidential cultivation of congressional leaders of both parties has often fostered a closer working relationship between Capitol Hill and the White House. President Kennedy, despite his differences with the GOP on many issues, always enjoyed a warm personal working relationship with GOP Senate Minority Leader Everett M. Dirksen. After Kennedy's assassination, President Johnson continued this same close relationship with Dirksen, even having a White House jetliner return Dirksen to Washington after a Florida vacation. Earlier, President Eisenhower had also found that his teamwork with Democratic Senate Majority Leader Lyndon Johnson and Speaker Sam Rayburn was often more productive than working with the Republican leader in the Senate.

President Truman tried to cater to Congress by bringing former lawmakers into his cabinet. At the outset he appointed former legislators as secretaries of state (James Byrnes), treasury (Fred M. Vinson), labor (Lewis Schwellenbach), and agriculture, (Clinton Anderson, then a congressman). In actuality, however, they were of little help to him in the field of domestic legislation because at the time Congress and the country were against the enactment of domestic reforms.

The failure of a President to take congressional leaders into his confidence can be a serious mistake—as President Nixon learned. His lack of prior consultations with congressional leaders, especially Senate Majority Leader Mike Mansfield (D.-Mont.) and Speaker Carl Albert (D.-Okla.), over his military intervention in Cambodia in 1970 created a deep sense of distrust on Capitol Hill. Eventually, Congress passed the War Powers Act of 1973 which aimed to halt future presidential intervention abroad. Still, Congress reserved the right to rescind presidential actions within this period by passing a concurrent resolution (which is not subject to presidential veto) to bring troops home. Likewise, President Nixon's miseries over the Watergate affair could be attributed, in part, to his failure to take congressional leaders, especially those of his own party, into his confidence. Only after Mr. Nixon's Gallup poll rating dropped to a new low, following the firing of Special Watergate Prosecutor Archibald Cox, did Mr. Nixon invite all Capitol Hill Republicans (in groups of 50 or more) to visit the White House to discuss the Watergate affair and what the President intended to do to reverse the lack of credibility in his administration.

International and Domestic Crises

Presidential-congressional cooperation has usually been close in times of international crises. President Truman's decision to send troops to Korea in 1950, President Eisenhower's dispatch of troops to Lebanon in 1958, President Kennedy's decision to blockade Cuba in 1962 after the discovery of Soviet missile sites on the island, and even President Johnson's retaliation against the North Vietnamese after the alleged Gulf of Tonkin incident temporarily generated broad congressional support for the President. However, the long-term American involvement in Vietnam eventually soured relationships between President Johnson (and later President Nixon) and "dovish" congressmen and senators.

Domestic crises have also brought the President and Congress closer together as partners in solving the nation's problems. In the midst of the Great Depression, President Franklin D. Roosevelt and Congress worked together to turn out an impressive volume of legislation, especially during the famous first "one hundred days" of FDR's first term. To be sure, Roosevelt enjoyed solid working majorities in both houses during this "honeymoon" period, but the willingness of Congress to rubber-stamp his stream of legislative proposals reflected the widespread belief on Capitol Hill that the President should be given all the tools necessary to combat the most severe depression in the country's history.[5] After the crisis had abated, Congress was less responsive to Roosevelt's initiatives. Indeed, during Roosevelt's second term, his New Deal legislative program lost much of its power. Except for passage of the Fair Labor Standards Act and the Agricultural Adjustment Act of 1938, the accomplishments of the second Roosevelt Administration were largely limited to consolidation of existing programs.

Despite his staggering problems with Congress over the Watergate affair, President Nixon found Congress warmly responsive to his special legislation message on the national energy crisis—an outgrowth of the 1973 Arab-Israeli War. Congress quickly endorsed several of his emergency energy conservation proposals and his request for standby authority to impose fuel and gas rationing. This teamwork came less than a week after Congress had sharply rebuffed the President by overriding his veto of the 1973 War Powers Act.[6]

Cooperation: Part Time Only

Though bridge-building between the President and Congress occurs frequently, the antipresidential vote on the War Powers Act of 1973 should alert the reader to the fact that the distance separating Capitol Hill and 1600 Pennsylvania Avenue on some issues can be calculated in miles, not blocks.

In any system of shared powers, such as exists between the President and Congress, an adversary relationship can be expected to develop from time to time. We have already mentioned some recent controversies between President Nixon and Congress—the congressional power of the purse versus presidential impoundment of appropriated funds, legislative oversight versus executive privilege, and the war-making power of the President versus the authority of Congress to limit foreign military intervention.

Executive-legislative conflict may also arise over local versus national interests and special interests versus general interests. Other conflict between the President and Congress often emerges between Democrats and Republicans, especially if one party controls the White House and the other controls one or both houses of Congress. From time to time, Presidents have also been engaged in legislative disputes with members of their own party. President Kennedy, despite his widespread popularity (a 1963 Gallup poll showed that 83 percent of the national sample said he was doing a good job in the White House), suffered several jolting legislative setbacks. Among his most conspicuous defeats were congressional rejection of an Urban Affairs Department, federal aid to public schools, income tax reform, medicare, and civil rights legislation. While Kennedy failed to win passage of these bills, all were subsequently approved after President Johnson's 1964 landslide victory over the conservative GOP nominee, Senator Barry Goldwater, which netted an additional 45 liberal northern Democratic congressmen—a solid "working" majority for LBJ.

President Kennedy's inability to win congressional approval of important segments of his domestic program revealed that the difference between a "voting" majority and a "working" majority in Congress can mean the difference between victory and defeat on key legislative measures. Although President Kennedy had a slight "voting" majority of Democrats in the House of Representatives, he in fact lacked a "working" majority, since many southern Democrats often voted against their own party's standard-bearer. As the young President pointed out, the decentralized party system in this country enabled a coalition of conservative southern Democrats and northern Republicans to thwart a presidential legislative program although each was a minority group. Special targets of his wrath were the congressional committee system and its seniority rule that enabled southern Democrats from one-party areas to control committee chairmanships and thereby congressional decision making. Kennedy deplored the fact that the congressional seniority system placed in key positions individuals who were wholly unsympathetic to his programs—even though they were members of his own party.

To overcome this lack of party discipline and the fragmented party system that enables congressmen to defy Presidents of their own party, some reformers have urged the establishment of a "responsible" party system. They insist that this reform would enable the President and the leader of the opposition party to offer the voters a clear-cut choice on the major public issues at election time. But this proposal conveniently overlooks the separation of powers system that fosters a divided government and a fragmented party system. Repeal of the separation of powers concept appears to be the only acceptable way to completely bridge the gap between the President and Congress. It is noteworthy that outright fusion of the executive and legislative powers was considered, and firmly rejected, by the founding fathers at Philadelphia in 1787, where both the Virginia and New Jersey plans contemplated the election of the President by Congress.

Since the prospects for overturning the existing constitutional structure with its independently elected President chosen for a specified term of office seem so remote at this time, we will turn our attention from the responsible parties proposal for the moment and concentrate on some of the less radical suggestions for overcoming executive-legislative deadlocks. Then we shall examine the new Hardin plan for a parliamentary system in the United States.

To better understand several of the proposals discussed in the following pages, a brief explanation of the parliamentary system

TABLE 7.1 Parliamentary Versus Presidential Systems

1. Parliament evolved from an Assembly which challenged the dominance of the Monarch.	1. Congress evolved from legislative branch under Articles of Confederation.

2. Executive is divided
   a) Head of Government—Prime Minister
   b) Head of State—ceremonial
	2. Executive is not divided—President is elected by people for a definite term.

3. Head of State appoints the Head of Government.	3. Head of Government is the Head of State.
4. Head of Government appoints the prime minister and Cabinet.	4. President appoints Cabinet who can not be members of Congress.
5. Cabinet consists of leading members of Parliament.	5. President is the sole executive.
6. Cabinet is politically responsible to the Parliament.	6. President is responsible to the electorate and the Constitution.
7. Prime minister asks the Head of State to dissolve Parliament.	7. President cannot dissolve Congress or threaten dissolution.
8. Parliament is supreme since there is no separation of power.	8. Congress is ultimately supreme, though it shares some functions and responsibilities with the President.
9. Cabinet is responsible to Parliament and only indirectly responsible to the electorate.	9. President is directly responsible to the electorate.
10. Checks and balances do not exist in parliamentary system.	10. Checks and balances are integral part of separation of powers.

Source: Douglas Verney, *Analysis of Political Systems* (London: Routledge and Kegan Paul, 1959), pp. 17–56.

---

is needed. In Table 7.1 the main features of the parliamentary and presidential systems are outlined and contrasted.

The main difference between the two systems is that under parliamentary government the legislature and executive are fused into one entity—the cabinet serves as the executive committee of the legislative branch and the prime minister as the leader. Under the presidential system, the chief executive is elected independently of the legislative branch by the national electorate for a specified term of office. The separation of powers divides responsibility between the President and Congress. Furthermore, the President must select his cabinet members from outside Congress; cabinet members are ineligible to serve simultaneously in either house of Congress. To help the reader, we have summarized the main features of the various proposed reforms of the presidential system in Table 7.2.

Proposals to Improve Presidential-Congressional Cooperation

Over the years more than a dozen proposals have been offered to facilitate cooperation between the coordinate branches of the national government on Capitol Hill and at 1600 Pennsylvania Avenue. In 1864 Representative George Pendleton (R.-Ohio) proposed that cabinet members be given seats in the House of Representatives with the privilege of entering debate and being present a certain number of days each month to answer questions. Senator Estes Kefauver, (D.-Tenn.) revised this plan for a question-and-answer period for department heads on the floor of either house. More recently, Senator Walter Mondale (D.-Minn.) offered the same proposal again.

Almost 20 years ago a leading authority on the presidency, Edward S. Corwin, suggested that more harmonious relations would develop between the President and Congress if the President would choose part of his cabinet from leading members of Congress. The restructured cabinet would be selected by the President from both houses of Congress. Added to this group would be as many executive department heads as were required by the nature of the activity.[7]

Another suggestion from academe is Professor Charles S. Hyneman's proposal to establish a central council to serve the President as an official advisory body. Members would be selected from the the congressional leadership, the President's own administrative staff, and individuals outside the government in whose judgment the President had confidence.[8] It might be noted that several states have established joint executive-legislative councils of the same general structure as those proposed by Corwin and Hyneman. Wisconsin, the originator of this idea, ended

TABLE 7.2 **Proposed Reforms**

Proposed Change	Effects upon Separation of Powers	Critique
Kefauver/Mondale—Question Period for Cabinet Members	No major alteration in present system	Presently accomplished in committee hearings. No major substantive improvement.
Corwin—Legislative Cabinet	Modified changes in present system	Ignores separate interest being represented in legislative and executive branches.
Hyneman—Legislative—Executive Council	Modified changes in present system	Ignores separate interest being represented in legislative and executive branches.
Finer—President and 11 Vice-Presidents with no confidence vote	Major changes in present system	Establishes parliamentary system in the U.S. that would require major changes in Constitution.
Reuss—No Confidence Vote	Major changes in present system	Constitutional amendment needed; President could become captive of shifting majorities in Congress.
Sundquist—No Confidence Vote	Major changes in present system	Parliamentary "no confidence" vote would require Constitutional amendment.
Hardin—Party Government	Major changes in present system	Would require major changes in constitutional structure; ignores decentralized party structure in the U.S.
Our Proposals	Maintain separation of powers	Permits executive leadership and innovation with Presidential accountability to the legislative branch.

its experiment after a brief trial. But Virginia has had greater success with its joint executive-legislative council.[9]

A far more radical departure—indeed almost a revolutionary proposal—is Professor Herman Finer's plan to elect a President and 11 Vice-Presidents together for a four-year term to serve as a kind of ministry through which the executive functions of government would be discharged. All 12 would be nominated together by national party conventions and elected for four years. The Congress would be elected at the same time for a four-year term. Under the Finer plan the President would preside over his cabinet or Vice-Presidents, assign them their respective jobs, dismiss any of them if he wished, and appoint others to their positions. Only persons who had served in Congress for at least four years would be eligible to run for the presidency or vice-presidencies. The President-elect and his cabinet or Vice-Presidents would be given full membership rights in the House of Representatives. The losing slate of cabinet candidates would be given seats in Congress and the duty of leading the "loyal opposition." If there were a vote of "no confidence," the President could (with the concurrence of a majority of his cabinet or Vice-Presidents) force the resignation of the entire team and thereby cause Congress to be dissolved. Then new elections would be held for all seats in Congress as well as for the President-Vice-President "cabinet."[10] Thus, the Finer plan would connect the executive and legislative branches through standard terms of office for the Congress and the cabinet.

Recently, Representative Henry Reuss (D.-Wis.) has proposed a constitutional amendment that would permit the ouster of a President by a "no confidence" vote. According to the Reuss plan, the House and Senate could vote "no confidence" in the chief executive by an extraordinary three-fifths majority. If this happened, the President would step aside at once. He would then be succeeded by the Vice-President—a member of his own party. The new President would serve until a special presidential election could be held within the next 90 to 110 days.

Representative Reuss' plan allows considerable flexibility on the time for the special election. If the "no confidence" vote came during the last year of a President's term, Congress could decide against a special election. If the "no confidence" vote occurred in a year of midterm congressional elections (for example, 1974 or 1978), the presidential election would simply be added to the congressional races. The President elected in this manner would assume office the following January and serve four years. If the special election occurred at any other time, Congress would specify when the new term would start, but it could not be less than 60 or more than 75 days following the election. The Reuss plan also contains a unique provision: an ousted President would be able to run again. The theory is that a defeated President should be given the opportunity to win vindication.[11] The two-term limitation of the 22nd Amendment would also be rescinded.

James L. Sundquist, a senior Fellow at the Brookings Institution, has also proposed to introduce an element of collective judgment into the exercise of executive power through a parliamentary vote of "no confidence," which could be implemented by a simple constitutional amendment. According to Sundquist, "The direct effect would be to make possible the removal of a President who, though not guilty of provable 'high crimes and misdemeanors' that are the basis for impeachment, has lost the capacity to lead and inspire and unify the country—in short the capacity to govern."[12] In the past, Sundquist points out, an incompetent President, surrounded by subordinates guilty of gross negligence, egregious mismanagement, or crimes and misdemeanors but who have acted in his name, "has remained in office until the end of his allotted four years—and nothing could be done about it." In Sundquist's view, "No other democratic government leaves itself so vulnerable."

If the "no confidence" vote were introduced into our Constitution, Sundquist contends, a President would have to do more than avoid indictable offenses. The merit of the parliamentary "no confidence" vote, Sundquist argues, would be that

> A President who was forced, under the Constitution to maintain the confidence of the country and of the Congress would find it necessary to consult with congressional leaders in the

exercise of his executive powers. He would not dare to do otherwise; it would be dangerous to flout them and risky to keep secrets from them. To retain their confidence, he would have to take them into his.[13]

One of the chief benefits of the "no confidence" vote, Sundquist believes, would be a rejuvenation of congressional leadership. As Sundquist puts it:

> The leaders of Congress would be in a position on crucial matters to make demands and say 'or else.' Major decisions would come to be taken in consultation. The executive power that the Founding Fathers reposed in the President alone would be on its way to being shared—checked and balanced. . . . The fundamental danger of rash or corrupting decisions taken by a lone President would to that extent be reduced.[14]

Sundquist is also certainly on sound ground when he observes:

> An institutional principle applied almost universally in the English-speaking world is that major decisions should be made not by one man acting *alone,* but by a collective body of some kind.[15]

One of the most provocative proposals to reform the existing system of divided government in the United States is the plan for "party government" offered by Professor Charles Hardin of the University of California at Davis. According to Hardin, "The foremost requirement of a great power is strong executive leadership." [16] But this executive must not be allowed to escape the political controls needed to maintain constitutional, that is, *limited* government. The problem is further complicated by the danger that restraints may seriously weaken the effectiveness of the President. Hardin's solution is "presidential leadership and party government." To achieve this goal, Hardin proposes a fundamental constitutional change in the American separation of powers system. This is how his new plan would be established:

1. Presidents, senators, and congressmen would all be elected for four-year terms. The election date would be fixed at four years from the date of the last inauguartion of the last government, but a provision would allow the government to change the date and call a special election.
2. The House of Representatives would continue to be elected from single-member districts, but an additional 150 members would be elected at large. To assure a majority in the House, each party would nominate 100 candidates; the party winning the presidency would elect its entire slate. The losing party would elect a maximum of at-large candidates, diminished by whatever number would be required to give the winning party a majority of five in the House. At-large candidates would be nominated by committees of 41 in each party. The winning party's committee would be composed of the President, the ten cabinet members, and 30 congressmen for single-member districts. The opposition party's nominating committee would be composed of the opposition party leader, the "shadow" cabinet (the opposition party leadership), and 30 congressmen. In both parties the 41-member nominating committee would have the right to reject local nominees if they had refused to accept party discipline.
3. Presidential candidates would be nominated by party committees composed of all house members from single-member districts as well as all candidates for election in such districts. In the event of either physical or political presidential disability, the nominating committee of his party would be empowered to suspend him temporarily or to remove him, but in any case it would be required to replace him. The office of Vice-President would be abolished.
4. The Senate would be deprived of its power to approve treaties and presidential nominations. Bills would continue to be considered in the Senate but if the Senate rejected a bill that had passed the House twice in the same form (60 days would have to elapse between the first and second passage), the bill would go to the President.

5. The presidential veto would be retained but it could be overridden by an adverse majority vote in the House. The Senate could require the House to reconsider but it could be overridden by the House after 60 days.
6. Article I, Section 6, Clause 2 of the Constitution, which prevents members of Congress from serving in other offices of the United States, would be repealed, but the similar office-holding ban for the judiciary would be retained.
7. The loser in the presidential election would be designated the leader of the opposition and given a seat in the House with privileged membership on all committees and privileged access to the floor. The opposition leader would have an official residence and adequate funds for office staff, travel, and other items essential for the vigorous operation of his office. Like the President, the opposition leader could be removed by his party's presidential nominating committee.
8. Presidential elections would be by national ticket. The winning party would be required to secure a national plurality of votes.
9. All parts of the Constitution which are presently in conflict with the foregoing proposals would be repealed or modified to conform to them. The 22nd Amendment (which limits the President to two terms) would also be repealed.

To the critics' charge that his plan is unrealistic and unworkable, Hardin's reply is that the existing system cannot cope with a politically disabled President who operates under a system of fixed calendar elections. To those opponents apprehensive of change, Hardin points out that all major Western democracies have undergone constitutional change in the past century. He reminds us that "Only the United States persists with constitutional forms essentially as they were devised nearly two hundred years ago."[17] Hardin argues that the party government system, which could provide party accountability and a smooth transition of presidential leadership, is preferable to the crippled system that now exists in this country.

Critique of Proposed Reforms

The Kefauver question-and-answer period, designed to encourage greater communication between Congress and the President, appears superficially to have merit. But upon closer examination it does not offer much substantive improvement. The Kefauver plan ignores the fact that the real business of Congress is transacted in its committees. Floor action consists largely of *pro forma* ratification of decisions agreed upon at the committee stage. Because heads of departments and agencies can testify before legislative committees and have ready access to committee members, the department heads already have a significant voice in the legislative process at the important committee stage. As one presidential observer has noted, "By the time an issue reaches the floor—if it reaches the floor—it is no longer an issue. It has been resolved." [18]

More plausible are the proposals for a joint executive-legislative council. Presumably, this council would offer a forum in which legislative compromises could be reached in a manner that would reduce presidential-congressional friction in the legislative process. But as Rowland Egger has observed, "The joint-council idea assumes a measure of discipline in the congressional party which the facts rarely justify, and it also ignores the enormous differences in the constituency of the President's congressional majority from one important administration measure to another." [19]

Corwin's proposal of a "legislative cabinet" to replace the presidential cabinet takes little account of the political facts of life governing the American separation of powers system. The legislative cabinet idea is an attempt to change the recognized ineffective advisory role of the cabinet as it is presently consituted. But the possibility of developing a viable advisory relationship between a President and cabinet composed of independently elected senators and congressmen who are firmly entrenched in a seniority system is extremely remote. Not only would this proposal weaken congressional political leadership, it would also undercut the President's independent sources of political authority. As the chief magistrate, the President can go over the heads of Congress and appeal directly to the people for support of his programs. By adroitly playing competing interest groups against each other and by appealing to the "national interest," the President has frequently achieved his goals, despite congressional foot-dragging. To force the President to surrender his initiative in both domestic and foreign affairs and to limit his goals to what he can "sell" to a legislative cabinet of senior members of the two houses would emasculate the President and leave him at the mercy of a congressional cabal. In addition, the legislative cabinet idea gives the President no more support or "clout" than he can secure at present by direct negotiation with his party leaders on Capitol Hill.[20]

Most intriguing of the reforms are the proposals for a modified British parliamentary system suggested by Finer and Hardin. As indicated earlier some of their proposals represent an attempt to revive ideas that were considered and rejected by the founding fathers. Proponents of the plural executive system seek to replace the President with an executive board having (a) collective responsibility and (b) the power to dissolve Congress. Other reformers believe that presidential-legislative friction could be eliminated if the President (by executive order) and the Congress (by concurrent resolution) were authorized by the Constitution to dissolve the government and call for simultaneous elections of the President, the Senate, and the House. These proposals have been formulated upon the mistaken belief that the threat of dissolution and general elections would bring the executive and legislative branches into agreement. But the advocates of a modified British parliamentary system ignore the fact that electoral power in the United States is completely decentralized. They apparently refuse to admit that national political parties are merely a loose confederation of 50 state parties that meets once every four years for the purpose of capturing the presidency. As presently organized, the national party has virtually no power to exert the type of disciplined authority necessary for the effective operation of a parliamentary system. Dissolution of Congress would pose no threat to congressmen and senators, because they owe their offices and allegiances to their district and state constituencies, not to the President or a cabinet. Consequently, as long as electoral power is organized on a state, or even a local basis, the President and Congress will have to rely upon compromise and negotiation, not structural changes, to achieve their legislative goals.

Does this mean, then, that our existing system must stagnate where it is? The founding fathers did not wish to create a system in which Congress and the President would erect fortifications from which each would launch frequent attacks against the other. But the authors of the Constitution firmly believed that a vigorous dialogue and even occasional skirmishes between Congress and the President could only serve to strengthen our system and make it more accountable to the people. Reassertion of congressional authority is indeed necessary if the excesses of the Johnson and Nixon Administrations are to be avoided in the future.

What Is to Be Done?

How can the Congress make the presidency more accountable to the American public? Several proposals immediately come to mind.

First, legislation to restrict the deployment of armed forces in overseas combat without congressional consent has already been enacted. A favorite presidential tactic of substituting executive agreements for treaties (which require senate ratification) must be sharply curtailed—unless it is made subject to congressional approval.

Second, both houses of Congress should establish standing committees on executive office operations. No longer can the job of overseeing presidential operations be divided among dozens of committees and subcommittees, each of which reviews only a small segment of the presidential establishment. The proposed standing committees would be charged specifically with overseeing White House operations. At first glance, this proposal may appear to add one more committee to the overworked congressional committee system. But few tasks are more crucial than overseeing the executive establishment and its 3 million employees. As presently organized, Congress is not adequately equipped to monitor the executive branch. Thomas E. Cronin has commented, "The presidency escapes with grievously inadequate scrutiny." [21] Public-minded legislators, helped by well-staffed committees, could conduct productive investigations that would advise Congress on alternative courses of action. Cronin reminds us that "Since the days of President Truman, Presidents have had staffs to oversee Congress [that is, congressional liaison staffs]; isn't it time for Congress to reciprocate?" [22] Senator Jacob Javits, too, has urged that every congressional committee should set up an executive liaison office to maintain communication with the executive department that the committee oversees to help guide the executive branch in transforming specific pieces of legislation into action.[23] Congress also needs these committees to counteract its own tendency to hand over to the presidency its diminishing resources and prerogatives. More reports and studies should be obtained from the executive branch on a regular basis.

Third, Congress should curb its habit of establishing new presidential agencies to deal with almost every new problem. By requiring the President to administer new programs through regular departments, Congress would be making its own contribution toward reducing the proliferation of executive agencies.

If Congress is to perform its sentry function over the executive establishment, it must make more generous use of the General Accounting Office (GAO). As the eyes and ears of Congress, the GAO has generally performed its auditing duties in adequate fashion. But it will need additional staffing if it is to assume expanded duties set forth by Congress.

Fourth, to increase presidential accountability, senate confirmation should be required for every important officer within the executive branch, including such powerful officers as the directors of the Office of Management and Budget, the Domestic Council, and the Council on International Economic Policy.[24]

If the awesome powers of the presidency are to be contained

within the law, Congress must ensure that "sensitive" agencies such as the FBI, CIA, and the Internal Revenue Service are not exploited for partisan (and corrupt) purposes—as was the case in the Watergate scandal. This can be achieved only by frequent congressional review of agency activities and budgets. Joint congressional committees should be established to share presidential authority over bureaus of intelligence and law enforcement. While one cannot remove all the dangers inherent in the inconsistency between democracy and a national police force, this proposal might help prevent future Watergate-type exploitation of these sensitive agencies. This proposal was advanced by Richard V. Goodwin, a former White House staffer during the Kennedy years, who says:

> It cannot be assumed that any congressional committee will prove a jealous guardian of civil liberties, but, if only from self-interest, a congressional group might be counted on to obstruct lawless acts intended to advance the political fortunes of the president and his party. Certainly it will increase the number of those who must be enlisted for illegal conspiracies.[25]

Fifth, the courts must, as the Supreme Court did recently in the historic decision, *United States* v. *Richard M. Nixon,* limit the use of the doctrine of executive privilege. While it is recognized that the President and his chief aides must be allowed to maintain confidentiality in communications on sensitive economic and security matters, Congress must also specify and set strict limits on the doctrine of executive privilege. As Cronin has pointed out, "Large numbers of unelected, unconfirmed, and unknown White House aides should not be allowed to hide behind the shield of executive privilege." [26] Congress should also clarify the term "national security" and make its application more precise so that the White House cannot stand behind this pretense whenever Congress questions specific decisions made in the Oval Office. President Ford's willingness to appear in person before a congressional subcommittee to answer questions about his pardoning of Richard M. Nixon will undoubtedly ease some of the public concern over the abuses of executive privilege.[27]

Sixth, the President should be required to report annually to the Congress on the steps he has taken to implement laws and resolutions passed by Congress during its previous session. Senator Javits' proposal that the President and cabinet officers should submit to questioning by a joint select committee of both houses also deserves serious consideration.[28]

Seventh, an independent prosecutor should be established, separate from the Justice Department, to prosecute alleged wrongdoing throughout the executive branch, including White House aides and the President of the United States. As the early stages of the Watergate cover-up investigation revealed only too well, no administration enthusiastically investigates wrongdoing within its own house. The brilliant work of Watergate Special Prosecutors Archibald Cox (who was fired by President Nixon) and Leon Jaworski has led to the conviction of more than a dozen White House aides, plus two cabinet members. Without congressional insistence that Watergate Special Prosecutor Leon Jaworksi could be removed only with the concurrence of congressional leaders, it seems highly unlikely that the Watergate conspirators would have been convicted—or that the Nixon impeachment inquiry would have ever gotten off the ground. As for the constitutional question that the creation of a permanent independent prosecutor, subject only to dismissal by Congress (or the courts) and not the executive, violates the separation of powers doctrine, Senator Birch Bayh (D.-Ind.), one of the original sponsors of this proposal, has rejoined:

> The separation of powers is not a formal, rigid doctrine dividing our government into watertight compartments. Rather, it is a functional doctrine to assure that checks and balances prevent one branch of government from assuming unreasonable powers. In the situation now confronting us [the Watergate cover-up investigation] it would do violence to this concept of the checks and balances to leave within the executive branch the authority for an investigation of the executive branch.[29]

These suggestions do not exhaust the list of proposals that could enable Congress to keep a checkrein on the President. The arsenal of congressional tools also includes the following: (1) rejection of a President's proposed legislation; (2) failure to confirm presidential nominees for high-level positions; (3) investigations or hearings, (4) addition of riders to appropriations legislation; (5) vetoing presidential reorganization plans.[30] Each of these tactics has been used from time to time, but to be effective they must be utilized far more systematically than they have been in recent decades. If this does not happen, the tactical advantages that Congress has recently enjoyed as a result of President Nixon's Watergate troubles and his threatened impeachment will gradually evaporate and the balance of power will swing back to the White House.

EFFECT OF WATERGATE AND IMPEACHMENT THREAT ON PRESIDENTIAL-CONGRESSIONAL RELATIONS

Just how deeply the Watergate affair had affected the presidency was evident for all to see in late November, 1973, when President Nixon, in response to a question about some alleged illegal deductions on his income tax returns, told a group of editors on a national television broadcast: "I've made my mistakes, but in all my years of public life I have never profited from public service . . . . I'm not a crook." [1] No other President in history has felt obligated to make such a pledge to the American public. Clearly, the Watergate affair had produced one of the swiftest transitions in the Washington power structure since the Civil War.

Switch in Presidential Posture

At a March 15, 1973, press conference, President Nixon flatly refused to permit his then-White House counsel John W. Dean, III, of subsequent Watergate fame, to testify at the confirmation hearings of L. Patrick Gray, III, who had been nominated to head the FBI. "I consider it my constitutional duty to defend the principle of the separation of powers," he declared, adding defiantly that he would welcome a Supreme Court test case on executive privilege—a case he was to lose in the historic decision of July, 1974. In foreign affairs Mr. Nixon was riding the crest of a success wave. In 1972 he became the first American President to visit mainland China, and his first visit to the Soviet Union was thought to mark the beginning of a new era of Soviet-American friendship. As leader of the world's strongest power, Mr. Nixon exuded unlimited confidence as he dealt with the great problems of war and peace.

Until the Watergate hearings, Mr. Nixon had claimed the right to wage unlimited war in Indochina. For example, in December, 1972, he decided unilaterally, without any consultation with congressional leaders, to unleash a ferocious, all-out bombing attack on North Vietnamese cities in an effort to achieve a cease-fire in Indochina.

The contrast in tone between President Nixon's 1973 and 1974 budget messages to Congress reflects how much the President's prestige and influence had waned in the intervening 12 months. President Nixon's 1973 budget message read more like a teacher's lecture to his students than a financial communication to a coequal branch of the government. The President, interpreting his 18 million-vote victory margin in the 1972 election as a mandate to direct and reorganize the federal government as he wished, demanded that Congress establish a rigid ceiling on spending—or he would do it himself.

A year later, reeling from the trauma of the Watergate affair, the President was far more conciliatory in addressing Congress. The mystique of his 1972 electoral mandate had virtually disappeared. The 1974 message did not renew his demand for a budget ceiling. Nothing was said about terminating federal programs and there was no more presidential impoundment of funds already appropriated by Congress.[3]

The marked shift from the belligerent tones of the 1973 message could be attributed mostly to the steady erosion of presidential popularity stemming from the Watergate scandals. During the intervening 12 months, Mr. Nixon had seen 26 staff members of the White House and the Committee to Re-Elect the President resign from office under a cloud of suspicion. More than a dozen of them were subsequently indicted and convicted for a list of crimes—perjury, obstruction of justice, illegal wiretapping, destruction of evidence, burglary, and so forth.

Congressional Renaissance

The opening sessions of the Senate Watergate Committee hearings pumped new confidence and determination into the lawmakers. In June, 1973, Congress no longer stood in awe of the President as it prepared for a last-ditch showdown over his Cambodian bombing policy. A major constitutional crisis between the President and Congress was averted by a last-minute compromise that allowed the President to continue bombing Cambodian rebel forces until August 15, 1973. By openly threatening to use the power of the purse to halt military spending for Cambodia, Congress warned Mr. Nixon that it was determined to share the war-making power in the future.

That Mr. Nixon clearly perceived this shift in the power balance was reflected shortly afterwards at a dedication speech in Pekin, Illinois, where he proclaimed a new "partnership" with Congress: "We can accommodate our positions without abandoning our principles." [4] Thus, after more than 40 years of the erosion of congressional prerogatives, a power shift was under way. The Cambodian confrontation was the first major victory for the newly revitalized Congress on the war-making issue. This reassertion of congressional authority by no means satisfied the lawmakers, who, after their summer recess, quickly passed the War Powers Act of 1973 and then overrode Mr. Nixon's veto of this legislation. An historic move by Congress, this new law compelled the President to consult with Congress when committing American forces overseas and to obtain congressional consent for any prolonged military action.

Sponsored originally by Senator Jacob Javits (R.-N.Y.), the War Powers Act was the culmination of three years' effort by Congress to agree on legislation that would prevent the country from slipping into another Vietnam-type war without the specific approval of Congress. The new law, declared Senator Javits, could mark an "historic turn" from the long-term trend toward arbitrary presidential war making, as well as a curb on the types of abuse of executive power disclosed by the Watergate hearings. The *New York Times* editorially reminded its readers, however, that "Congress has always possessed powers that are spelled out for it in the bill. What has been lacking has been the courage and will to exercise that power rationally in the face of the emotional pressures generated by a President and his military advisers in times of crisis, real or imagined." [5] And the *Times'* editorial was not stretching the point when it emphasized that the Javits' bill "actually concedes to the President more power than the Founding Fathers ever contemplated, judging by the debates at the Constitutional Convention." Indeed, the same editorial recalled that "Even Alexander Hamilton, the leading exponenet of a powerful Presidency, held that the initiation of a state of war 'is the peculiar and exclusive province of Congress.' " [6]

On the domestic front, Mr. Nixon's attacks on congressional "fiscal irresponsibility" and "budget-busting" spending triggered another congressional counterattack to reclaim decision-making power over the federal budget, a power that had passed to the White House through congressional indifference and disorganization.

With the passage of the Congressional Budget and Impoundment Control Act of 1974, Congress, for the first time in more than half a century, has become an active partner of the White House in drawing up a federal budget, instead of merely approving or refusing presidential proposals or developing its own isolated and improvised programs.[7] Because the rate of inflation, the level of income taxes, the size of the national debt, and the price of bread are all affected by the size and shape of the national budget, Senator Charles Percy is probably accurate in predicting that the new budget act will be "one of the historic turning points in the evolution of our institutions." [8]

Congress has been aided in reestablishing itself as a coequal branch of the government by the succession of Watergate-connected revelations that tarnished Mr. Nixon directly: his questionable tax deduction on his vice presidential papers that resulted in his belated $467,000 tax bill; the use of more than $10 million in federal government funds to improve the physical security of his Florida and California residences; the subpoenaing of the White Houses tapes by Special Prosecutor Leon Jaworski and the House Judiciary Committee; and the $100,000 Howard Hughes campaign contribution that is alleged to have been distributed to his personal secretary, Rose Mary Woods, his two brothers, and "other unnamed sources." But the most effective instrument for "cutting the President down to size" and restoring a constitutional balance between the executive and legislative branches was the presidential impeachment inquiry launched by the House Judiciary Committee in late October, 1973.

Growing Threat of Impeachment against President Nixon

Spawned by the White House cover-up of the Watergate scandals, the house impeachment inquiry had mushroomed by January, 1974, to include the following charges against Mr. Nixon: the payment of "hush" money to Watergate defendant, E. Howard Hunt; curtailing the FBI investigation of the break-in; subverting the CIA to help cover the tracks of the Watergate defendants; destroying evidence of the establishment of a special White House secret police unit—the so-called "plumbers" group—that broke into Daniel Ellsberg's psychiatrist's office; attempted bribery of the federal judge in the Ellsberg "Pentagon Papers" case by asking if the judge would be interested in the directorship of the FBI during the course of the trial; alleged bribery in the International Telephone and Telegraph and the Associated Milk Producers, Inc. campaign donations to the GOP; subverting constitutional rights with the "Huston plan" for surveillance of critics and political enemies; the 1969 wiretapping of more than a dozen White House aides and newsmen without warrants; and ordering a bombing campaign in Cambodia in 1969 and 1970 without congressional authorization.

The first task of the House Judiciary Committee was to determine if these actions constituted sufficient grounds for drawing up a "bill of impeachment" to be presented to the full House for a vote. Though the word impeachment is mentioned in several parts of the Constitution, relatively few Americans were familiar with the term before the Nixon impeachment inquiry. What is this unique provision that the founding fathers deliberately placed in the Constitution to remove a President from office or to adjudge his innocence of "high crimes and misdemeanors"?

Impeachment: The Ultimate Check

Though seldom used, impeachment is the most awesome power in the Constitution. What are the grounds for impeachment? The Constitution (Article II, Section 4) states that a President may be impeached for "treason, bribery, or other high crimes and misdeameanors." Treason and bribery are well-defined offenses, but there is wide disagreement as to what constitutes "other high crimes and misdemeanors." President Nixon's lawyers and many Republicans in the House and Senate argued that a President can be impeached only for indictable offenses—charges that can be sustained in a criminal trial. This can be termed "the strict constructionist" theory of impeachment.

A second theory is that an impeachable offense is what a majority of the members of the House of Representatives says it is. This might be termed the "Jerry Ford" theory, since then House Minority Leader Jerry Ford, leader of the forces seeking to impeach Supreme Court Justice William Douglas in 1970, declared, "An impeachable offense is whatever the majority of the House of Representatives considers it to be at a given moment in history." [9] This interpretation suggests a system in which the ultimate authority of the presidency depends not on a national election, but on a majority vote in Congress.

The third theory of impeachment—based on a broad interpretation of "other high crimes and misdemeanors"—includes political offenses as well as indictable crimes. This position has been espoused by one of the leading authorities on impeachment, Professor Raoul Berger of Harvard University. He argues that in early English history the term "high crimes and misdemeanors" had a specific meaning of which the founding fathers were clearly aware. English law, according to Berger, defined "high crimes and misdemeanors" as subversion of the Constitution, abuse of power, neglect of duty, or betrayal of trust. According to Berger, "None of these offenses—the very offenses which those who framed the Constitution wished to guard against—have ever been indictable offenses." [10] Because of the fixed length of presidential terms, Berger says, the authors of the Constitution intended that impeachment serve as a means of removing the chief executive for bad conduct. As Berger puts it, "The Founders conceived impeachment chiefly as a 'bridle' upon the President and his coadjusters."[11] And Berger continues, "It was because the separation of powers left no room for removal by a vote of no confidence that impeachment was adopted as a safety valve, a security against an oppressive or corrupt President and his sheltered ministers."[12] The impeachment process, Berger noted, is the one constitutional bridge in the separation of powers doctrine. That is, a President cannot avoid an impeachment charge merely by arguing that the congressional inquiry invades his executive domain guaranteed by the Constitution.[13]

The framers, Berger reminds us, "completely separated the impeachment removal proceedings from a subsequent indictment and criminal trial."[14] As further proof, Berger points out that the framers included the double jeopardy amendment and the sixth amendment provision for trial by jury "in all criminal prosecutions" as additional constitutional safeguards for impeached defendants in subsequent court trials.

Lawyers for the House Judiciary Committee, which was investigating possible grounds for impeaching President Nixon in early 1974, espoused the broad or liberal interpretation of impeachment. In a 49-page advisory report to committee members entitled "Constitutional Grounds for Presidential Impeachment," the bipartisan staff flatly rejected arguments that a President was subject to impeachment only for indictable criminal offenses. According to the judiciary committee lawyers, the impeachment process is a "constitutional safety valve" designed to protect the nation from "grave misconduct."[15] Impeachment, the report continued, is a remedy against "constitutional wrongs that subvert the structure of government, or undermine the integrity of office and even the Constitution itself." The committee report indicated that a President could be impeached on such noncriminal grounds as dereliction of duty or failure to comply with the Constitution's mandate to "take care that the laws be faithfully executed." Limiting impeachable conduct to criminal offenses, the report noted, would be "incompatible" with the history of impeachment and the intent of the Constitution's authors.

In several places, the judiciary committee memorandum suggested that President Nixon might be subject to impeachment for the criminal acts of his subordinates in the Watergate break-in and cover-up. To reinforce this point, the committee staff lawyers cited the argument of one of the Constitution's authors, James Madison, that a President could be impeached for permitting subordinates "to perpetrate with impunity high crimes or misdemeanors against the United States, or neglects [*sic*] to superintend their conduct, so as to check their excesses." [16] Whether a President can be held responsible and impeached for his subordinates' illegal activity is, however, a "gray area" in the impeachment process that will have to await further interpretation by the House Judiciary Committee, and very likely, the full House.

The New York City Bar Association's 1974 report on impeachment also gives a liberal interpretation to the impeachment proceeding:

> . . . the grounds for impeachment are not limited to or synonymous with crimes (indeed, acts constituting a crime may not be sufficient for the impeachment of an office holder in all circumstances). Rather, we believe that acts which undermine the integrity of government are appropriate grounds whether or not they happen to constitute offenses under the general criminal law.[17]

The report alludes to the kinds of acts which could meet this test. They include "acts which constitute corruption in or flagrant abuse of the powers of official position." Impeachable offenses, the report continues,

> . . . may also be found in acts which, without directly affecting government processes undermine that degree of public confidence in the probity of executive and judicial offices that is

essential to the effectiveness of government in a free society. . .[18]

In essence, the report concludes that impeachment proceedings constitute a decision by the two houses of Congress "that the office holder has demonstrated by his actions that he is unfit to continue in the office in question."

As indicated earlier, President Nixon and his lawyers made a strong argument that he could be impeached only for indictable offenses—charges which they believed two-thirds of the U.S. Senate would not sustain. A week after the publication of the House Judiciary Committee's report on impeachment, the White House legal staff released its own 61-page analysis of the constitutional standards required for presidential impeachment. Attorneys for Mr. Nixon concluded that the Constitution requires not only criminal conduct but also criminal acts of "a very serious nature" to provide grounds for impeaching a President.[19]

Citing many of the same sources used by the Judiciary Committee's legal staff, the White House lawyers reported, "The evidence is conclusive on all points: a President may only be impeached for indictable crimes." Mr. Nixon's lawyers argued that to conclude otherwise would expose the executive branch to the threat of "political impeachments." The White House legal staff pointed out that in its later years the English impeachment process was used as a weapon by the legislative branch to win supremacy over the executive. The White House lawyers rejected many of the precedents in English law cited by the judiciary committee staff with these words:

> To argue that the President may be impeached for something less than a criminal offense, with all the safeguards that definition implies would be a monumental step backwards into all those old English practices that our Constitution sought to eliminate. American impeachment was not designed to force a President into surrendering executive authority but to check overtly criminal actions as they are defined by law.[20]

In American history, the White House lawyers maintained, only the impeachment of President Andrew Johnson should be considered for guidance. Other impeachment proceedings, dealing almost exclusively with federal judges, are not enlightening because judges are not removable by the elective process as are Presidents, the study reported.

The White House lawyers concluded that "The most salient lesson to be learned from the Johnson trial is that impeachment of a President should be resorted to only for cases of that gravest kind—the commission of a crime named in the Constitution or a criminal offense against the laws of the United States." [21]

In still another report on impeachment compiled by the Justice Department, the Office of Legal Counsel announced its agreement with what is considered the view of the majority of legal scholars, who hold that once a President is impeached by the House and convicted by the Senate, the courts cannot review the decision. As noted by the legal staff of the Justice Department, the unavailability of judicial review presents another argument for basing impeachment on political acts rather than on criminal acts.[22]

In any event, legal scholars seem to be in general agreement on one point: an impeachable offense must be serious in nature.

The Nixon Impeachment Inquiry

The impeachment inquiry against President Nixon began rather slowly in late October, 1973. Although impeachment had been in the back of the minds of many observers since it was first indicated that the Watergate burglary implicated the White House, the Nixon impeachment inquiry did not become a reality until a week after the "Saturday night massacre"—Mr. Nixon's firing of the Watergate Special Prosecutor, Archibald Cox, and the resignations of Attorney General Elliot Richardson and his deputy, William Ruckelshaus. Within a week, a torrent of 350,000 telegrams from irate citizens (the largest number ever received by Western Union in Washington during a seven-day period), descended on Capitol Hill. The vast majority called for the resignation or impeachment of Mr. Nixon.

The movement toward an impeachment inquiry began in earnest in mid-November, 1973, when the House of Representatives appropriated $1 million for the Judiciary Committee to hire a special counsel and staff.

In early February, 1974, the House voted 410 to 4 to grant the Judiciary Committee broad subpoena power to investigate President Nixon's conduct. For only the second time in the nation's history, the House empowered the committee to subpoena anyone, including the President, for evidence pertinent to the investigation.[23] The only previous investigation of a President's conduct had occurred in 1867, when the House adopted a similar resolution directing the Judiciary Committee to investigate the possible impeachment of Andrew Johnson. However, no subpoenas were issued against Johnson.

During this early phase of the impeachment inquiry, House Speaker Carl Albert, (D.-Okla.), predicted confidently that a vote would be taken by the full House, even if the House Judiciary Committee did not recommend impeachment.[24] His reasoning was based on the fact that according to house rules, impeachment resolutions are highly privileged, and a member may demand a vote on impeachment at any time. Just as Robert's *Rules of Order* gives precedence to a motion for adjournment, house rules require that an impeachment vote, if demanded, be given immediate consideration. Father Robert F. Drinan (D-Mass.), a priest who had opposed the Vietnam War, and at least two other members of the House had submitted impeachment resolutions in the fall of 1973 and were prepared to offer them at a propitious moment. Therefore, it was a question of *when,* not *if,* the house vote would be taken.

Throughout the spring and early summer of 1974, the Nixon impeachment inquiry appeared bogged down in endless debate and partisan wrangling over such points as whether President Nixon's counsel, James St. Clair, should be allowed to listen to all the nonpublic proceedings (he was), the list and number of witnesses to be called, and whether the hearings should be public or in executive session, with the public and press excluded. President Nixon publicly displayed his lack of concern over the proceedings by scheduling special tours to the Middle East and the Soviet Union. While Mr. Nixon basked in the televised limelight as more than a million Egyptians surrounded his caravan in Cairo as he exchanged greetings with Prime Minister Anwar Sadat, and while he exchanged toasts in Moscow with Soviet Premier Leonid Brezhnev over the recently established Soviet-American détente, the President seemed to have slowed down the impeachment tide. After he returned to Washington, President Nixon continued to defy the Judiciary Committee's eight separate subpoenas, issued between February and May, 1974, for 147 separate taped White House conversations by invoking the doctrine of executive privilege.[25] James St. Clair argued that the President had a constitutional right to maintain the confidentiality of White House conversations; otherwise, he asserted, the President would be denied the opportunity to engage in private discussions and to obtain candid advice on matters of state.

However, Mr. Nixon was dealt a shattering defeat on the issue of executive privilege by the U.S. Supreme Court in late July, 1974. By a vote of 8 to 0, the high court flatly rejected the President's contention of absolute executive privilege, and ruled that President Nixon must provide potential evidence (White House electronic tapes, transcripts, papers, and memoranda) for the impending criminal trial of his former subordinates.[26] Although the case did not hinge on the House Judiciary Committee's subpoenas of White House tapes—which Mr. Nixon continued to ignore—the magnitude of his defeat echoed throughout the nation and ultimately sealed his fate. Specifically, the Court's ruling involved Special Watergate Prosecutor Leon Jaworski's request for 64 taped White House conversations between Mr. Nixon and several of his top aides who had been charged in the Watergate cover-up conspiracy. Because several previously subpoenaed White House tapes had subsequently been turned over to the House Judiciary Committee by the special prosecuter, the supposition on Capitol Hill was that these 64 tapes would also

Effect of Watergate

become available for the anticipated Nixon impeachment trial.

President Nixon waited eight hours after the Supreme Court's verdict before Mr. St. Clair read a statement to the press announcing that Mr. Nixon would comply with the decision "in all respects." [27] Until this announcement was made the nation had wondered if the President would accept a ruling by the high court limiting his use of executive privilege.

However, the House Judiciary Committee did not wait for new evidence to emerge as a result of the Supreme Court's decision. It moved ahead the same day with its final debate on recommending a senate trial of the President for alleged misconduct in office.

The final six days of the Judiciary Committee's hearings, carried on nationwide television, permitted millions of Americans to witness a debate which would decide the fate of the President of the United States. For most of these viewers, it was the first time that they had seen a congressional committee in action, much less an impeachment proceeding. Once the House Judiciary Committee opened its session to network television and the press, President Nixon's hope of avoiding a house impeachment vote began to fade. The impact of the committee's hearings on Mr. Nixon's chances of surviving an impeachment vote was devastating. As one veteran reporter noted, "With the assistance of television, the committee did much to ruin the climate for the kind of counterattacks on which the White House has relied almost since the advent of the Watergate scandals more than two years ago." [28] The White House charges that the Judiciary Committee was acting like a "kangaroo court" fell on deaf ears, as the viewers heard the most impassioned defenders of the President compliment the judiciary committee chairman, Democrat Peter Rodino of New Jersey, on the evenhandedness of his rulings and the fairness of the procedures he had devised.

Within a week of the Supreme Court's historic decision on executive privilege, the House Judiciary Committee, by votes of 27 to 11, 28 to 10, and 21 to 17, recommended three articles of impeachment against President Nixon. The three articles charged that Mr. Nixon had obstructed justice in the Watergate burglary cover-up, abused his authority in violation of his oath of office to uphold the Constitution, and subverted the Constitution by seeking to impede the impeachment process by defying eight committee subpoenas for 147 recorded White House conversations.[29] During the final debate the Committee rejected two other impeachment articles. One involved President Nixon's secret bombing of Cambodia in 1969-70; the second concerned Mr. Nixon's questionable deductions on his income tax returns.

Faced with the prospect of almost certain impeachment by the House of Representatives, as more Republican congressmen deserted the sinking presidential ship, President Nixon resigned from office on August 9, 1974—the first President to give up the office.

The President's Diminishing Options

Prior to President Nixon's resignation he weighed several options still open to him before the full House of Representatives considered the articles of impeachment. Let's take a brief look at his choices.

House Bypass Plan Less than a day after the House Judiciary Committee approved the three articles of impeachment, White House officials reported that President Nixon was considering a shift of strategy, in which he would try to bypass an impeachment debate in the House of Representatives and take his case directly to the Senate for quick resolution. According to Patrick J. Buchanan, a special assistant to the President, Mr. Nixon had "not ruled out" a plan whereby he would ask the House to vote unanimously for his impeachment without debate, so that he could speedily face a trial in the Senate. With a two-thirds vote required to convict in the Senate (but only a majority vote needed to adopt articles of impeachment in the House), Mr. Nixon felt that his chances for survival were much better in the Senate.

First proposed by Representative Louis Frey (R.-Fla.), the House Bypass Plan was viewed by some White House aides as a means of taking the impeachment procedure out of the House in one dramatic stroke in order to allow the clamor for impeachment to subside. The White House disclosure that the President was considering the House Bypass Plan represented a sudden shift from the statement heard repeatedly during the House Judiciary Committee proceedings that Mr. Nixon was "absolutely" confident that the House would reject articles of impeachment. A number of influential Republican congressmen, however, indicated that the President's request to adopt the House Bypass Plan would be refused. House GOP Conference Leader John B. Anderson of Illinois bitterly complained, "Certainly we are intended to be more than a letter-drop where you deposit these (impeachment) articles on the way to the Senate." [31]

Censure In early August, 1974, a group of Republican congressmen proposed an alternative to Mr. Nixon's impeachment; they recommended a vote of censure. Representative Paul Findley (R.-Ill.), introduced a resolution which would charge that Mr. Nixon was guilty of "negligence, moral insensitivity, and maladministration" and should therefore be censured. Whether or not the White House supported this move could not be determined at the time.

Proponents of the censure motion acknowledged that they had little chance of prevailing, but they said that at least the censure motion offered the troubled members a choice. It appeared unlikely that the Democratic-controlled Rules Committee would allow floor debate on any censure motion during the house impeachment debate. Speaker Carl Albert (D.-Okla.), said he would oppose the Findley resolution "because it's not material to the issue." [33]

Resignation President Nixon had said on several occasions, "I have no intention whatever of ever walking-away from the job that the people elected me to do." But the possibility of his resignation should not have been ruled out. Former Vice-President Agnew's repeated assertion, "I will never resign," was followed by his sudden resignation after it was revealed that he had accepted political kickbacks and had failed to pay income tax on this money. Therefore, the thought of presidential resignation was not that improbable.

The founding fathers were not unmindful of the possibility of resignation. Article II of the Constitution reads:

> In case of the removal of the President from office, or of his death, resignation, or inability to discharge the powers and Duties of the said office, the same shall devolve on the Vice President, and the Congress may by law provide for the Case of Removal, Death, Resignation, or Inability both of the President and Vice President, declaring what officer shall then act as President, and such officer shall act accordingly, until the Disability be removed, or a President shall be elected.

The 25th Amendment also provides for the possibility of resignation. Section 1 reads: "In case of the removal of the President from office or his death or resignation, the Vice President shall become President."

As the unraveling of the Watergate affair touched ever closer to the President in the fall of 1973 and the spring of 1974, attention turned frequently to the possibility of President Nixon's resignation. This was not the only instance in recent times in which the topic of presidential resignation had been raised. In 1946, following the congressional elections in which the Democrats lost control of Congress for the first time in 16 years, Senator J. William Fulbright (D.-Ark.) urged President Truman to resign for the good of the country.[34] Truman, however, crustily rejected the suggestion and marched on to reelection in 1948, winning back Democratic control of both houses.

The frequency of resignation talk increased after House Minority Leader Gerald Ford was confirmed as the new Vice-President in late 1973. Republican lawmakers were now willing to discuss the possibility of Mr. Nixon's resignation more openly, since there was no longer any fear that Democratic House Speaker Carl Albert would succeed to the presidency, as there was during the period in which the vice-presidency was vacant (October 10 to December 6, 1973). Senator Edward Brooke (R.-Mass.) was the first GOP legislator to ask for Mr. Nixon's resignation. And while only a handful of GOP lawmakers were willing at that time to declare publicly that they favored Mr. Nixon's resignation, it was common knowledge on Capitol Hill that a growing number of GOP congressmen (all facing reelection) and many of those GOP senators up for reelection were anxious to have President Nixon step down because they considered him a political albatross around their necks. Democratic lawmakers, anxious to capitalize politically from the threatened impeachment of Mr. Nixon, and considering a possible Democratic landslide in the 1974 elections if Mr. Nixon were still "wallowing in Watergate," seemed less inclined to push for a quick resignation. However, Representative Wilbur Mills (D.-Ark.), Chairman of the powerful Ways and Means Committee, twice indicated his willingness to introduce a bill guaranteeing Mr. Nixon full immunity from all future court indictments if he were to resign.[35] Mr. Nixon spurned Mills' offers.

Although President Nixon had vowed repeatedly that he would never resign, there were powerful financial and legal reasons for him to do so. As long as Mr. Nixon was confident that that at least 34 senators would support him, he had little or nothing to gain by resigning. But once he was faced with a possible impeachment conviction and the end of his presidency, the following dollars-and-cents factors helped persuade him to step down: (a) He would, if removed, automatically lose his lifetime pension of $60,000 a year; (b) he would forfeit Mrs. Nixon's right to a widow's pension of $20,000 a year; (c) he would be denied $96,000 a year provided by Congress for staff salaries, allowances, and free office space for the rest of his life.[36] Mr. Nixon apparently weighed all these factors carefully before he tendered the following statement to Secretary of State Henry Kissinger on August 9, 1974:

"I hereby resign the office of President of the United States."
25th Amendment "Leave of Absence" Under the 25th Amendment, ratified in 1967, Mr. Nixon could have taken a temporary "leave of absence" during the impeachment inquiry, turning over the reins of government to then Vice-President Gerald R. Ford until the impeachment question was resolved. Section 3 of the 25th Amendment reads:

> Whenever the President transmits to the President pro tempore of the Senate and the Speaker of the House of Representatives his written declaration that he is unable to discharge the powers and duties of his office, and until he transmits to them a written declaration to the contrary, such powers and duties shall be discharged by the Vice President as Acting President.

Thus, Vice-President Ford could have served as Acting President during the impeachment proceedings. If Mr. Nixon had been found innocent of the impeachment charges, he could have resumed his presidential duties upon formal notification to the president pro tempore of the Senate and the Speaker of the House of Representatives. If Mr. Nixon had been found guilty of impeachable offenses by a two-thirds vote of the Senate, he would have of course been removed from office, and Mr. Ford would have officially become President of the United States. Although the procedures outlined here have never been used, most legal experts believe that the idea of an Acting President represents a viable alternative to presidential resignation. In early May, 1974, Senator Milton Young (R.-N. Dak.), a conservative and one of Mr. Nixon's staunchest defenders in the Senate, was the first discontented GOP senator to urge Mr. Nixon to "take the 25th Amendment" and step aside until his name could be cleared of any wrongdoing.[37]

Following the House Judiciary Committee's decisive, bipartisan vote for articles of impeachment in late July, 1974, the suggestion was revived on Capitol Hill that President Nixon use the 25th Amendment and make Vice-President Ford the acting President during the impeachment proceedings. Supporters of this course of action agreed that President Nixon could not be expected to defend himself against the impeachment charges and perform his broad executive duties at the same time. But at no time before his resignation did Mr. Nixon give any indication that he planned to use the 25th Amendment and step aside temporarily.

As Mr. Nixon fought a disorganized rearguard action against the pro-impeachment forces, a Harris poll taken in early August,

1974, reported that 66 percent of the American people believed "the House of Representatives should vote to impeach President Nixon so he can be tried by the U.S. Senate." [38] Before the House Judiciary Committee had voted to adopt articles of impeachment, 53 percent had favored impeachment.

Nixon Yields to Congress on Other Fronts

While the impeachment drive against Mr. Nixon dominated the news, a shift in presidential-congressional power relations was evident on several fronts. For example, President Nixon reversed his long-asserted conviction that White House aides are not subject to the same congressional scrutiny as cabinet officers and others whose appointments are confirmed by the Senate. Shortly before the House Judiciary Committee voted articles of impeachment, Mr. Nixon agreed to permit Kenneth Rush, his counselor for economic policy, to testify before congressional committees. Even before passage of the Congressional Budget and Impoundment Control Act of 1974, President Nixon had abandoned his earlier policy of impounding funds already appropriated by Congress. Much of this impoundment activity was not as concerned with fiscal restraint as it was with allocating federal resources according to the administration's views. In addition, Mr. Nixon stopped issuing executive orders to end social welfare programs supported by Congress. Mr. Nixon also shelved his plan to reshape broad areas of governmental policy without congressional authority and to effect important foreign and domestic policies without congressional participation.

TOWARD A NEW POLITICAL ORDER

Will the end of the Watergate affair, the House impeachment inquiry, and Richard Nixon's subsequent resignation bring a return to executive dominance over the legislative branch? Can Congress reestablish a permanent balance of power that will enable the lawmakers to compete with the President on equal terms in policy making?

Most Washington observers perceived a definite swing away from presidential dominance of the American governmental system during the extended Watergate hearings. The decline in presidential influence was most notable in the area of the President's duties as commander-in-chief. The congressional decision to cut off all funds for U.S. bombing raids against Cambodian rebel forces after August 15, 1973, was the first major legislative curtailment of the presidential war-making activities during the long American involvement in Indochina. More important for its long-range impact was congressional passage, over President Nixon's veto, of the 1973 War Powers Act. A few critics, for example, Senator Thomas Eagleton (D.-Mo.), argued that the new law actually expanded rather than restricted the President's war-making activities. But the prevailing congressional view was that the original intent and impetus for the War Powers Act of 1973 was to control presidential power, not to enlarge it.

In 1972 Congress had begun a movement to curtail the President's largely unrestricted actions in foreign affairs, especially the widespread use of executive agreements. The Case bill, which was enacted into law, requires the President to furnish Congress with a list of all executive agreements employed to secure military bases and the storage of U.S. nuclear weapons abroad. Senator Clifford Case (R.-N.J.) also introduced an amendment to the military foreign aid bill to prohibit the use of federal funds in any future executive agreement for military base rights overseas, unless the arrangement is approved by the Senate as a treaty.[1] However, this amendment failed to win congressional approval.

The agenda for structural reform of executive-legislative relationships, however, will require determined action by Congress on the domestic front. At first glance it would appear much easier for Congress to clamp down on presidential power in domestic matters, because the Constitution grants the President broad latitude in dealing with such foreign relations questions as recognition of nations, the exchange of ambassadors, and the negotiation of treaties. Yet the rebalancing of executive-legislative power in the field of domestic policy has not moved as quickly or as easily as some presidential critics had hoped. One reason is that the 535 members of Congress seem unable to act quickly or decisively. Frequently it is simply a case of "too many cooks in the kitchen." Jealous committee chairmen, anxious to protect their prerogatives, have been unwilling to act. At times, jealousy between the House and Senate has also inhibited action. Thus, in May, 1973, when the house sustained a presidential veto of a bill that would have required senate confirmation of the current director of the Office of Management and Budget, some house members explained their vote as a refusal to give the Senate any additional power.[2]

The Dilemma of Power

Since the founding of the Republic, we have been faced with a never-ending dilemma: How do we permit strong executive action and still keep the presidency accountable? If the power of the presidency cannot be reduced appreciably—and in a fast-moving, complex world filled with tension, it probably should not be—what are our choices? The supreme irony of the recent congressional counterattack against executive usurpation of the lawmakers' prerogatives is that while Congress sought to prune White House powers born of past crises—for example, the passage of the 1973 War Powers Act—the legislators were also in the process of granting President Nixon new emergency authority to deal with the critical energy shortage. Indeed, the President now presides over the greatest accumulation of federal power that peacetime America has ever known. Thus, while Congress has sought to curtail presidential power in foreign affairs in the past year the lawmakers have authorized the chief executive to issue edicts that set the price of a loaf of bread and a gallon of gasoline, banned outdoor Christmas tree lighting, regulated the setting of living room thermostats, and encompassed numerous other restrictions formerly left to the decisions of individual citizens. The dilemma facing Congress is not new: on the one hand, there is a need for quick executive action to deal with urgent national problems; on the other hand, many congressmen want to guard the congressional prerogatives of power of the purse and legislative oversight.

Recently, the House Commerce Committee took note of this underlying dilemma in its report on the energy bill: ". . . Congress has repeatedly been presented with the problem of finding a means by which a legislative body in a democratic republic may extend extraordinary powers for use by the executive branch during times of great crisis without imperiling our constitutional balance of liberty and authority." [3]

A young, conservative congressman, Barry M. Goldwater, Jr., (R.-Calif.), warned his colleagues: ". . . it does us little good to attempt to regain congressional prerogatives in foreign affairs with the war powers bill, and then turn right around and hand the President a domestic 'Gulf of Tonkin' in the name of an emergency crisis." [4] This pattern is familiar to most Washington observers: when the pressure mounts, the lawmakers on Capitol Hill have a habit of delegating authority and looking to the White House for action.

As indicated earlier, a special committee of the U.S. Senate, jointly chaired by Senators Frank Church (D.-Ida.) and Charles Mathias (R.-Md.) studied existing presidential emergency powers for the purpose of repealing some of them. Committee members discovered that since the first declared state of emergency in 1933, Congress has passed more than 470 laws delegating emergency authority to the executive branch.[5] Yet senators and congressmen never cease complaining that this emergency legislation delegates unprecedented, dangerous authority to the President. They warn that a stroke of the chief executive's pen can cause drastic alterations to the personal and business lives of millions of Americans. Nevertheless, swift action must be taken to deal with national crises. The lawmakers have yet to find a satisfactory solution to this dilemma of power.

Lessons of Watergate, the Impeachment Inquiry, and the Nixon Resignation

In an era of continuing international crises, the threat of an "executive dictatorship" is always lurking in the shadows. Representative John Seiberling (D.-Ohio) undoubtedly had this thought in mind during the House Judiciary Committee's impeachment proceedings when he asked: "If the Founding Fathers were concerned with the abuse of power by a chief executive in a small fledgling country, how much more would they be concerned today when the president . . . holds the power of life and death over the people of this country and indeed the entire world."[6]

As millions of Americans watched the presidential impeachment proceedings on television, they may have reached the same conclusion reached by a majority of House Judiciary Committee members, namely, that the impeachment power—the ultimate check and balance in our form of government—has operated to preserve and strengthen the American system in a way that the framers of the Constitution intended.

If there is but one lesson to be learned from the trauma of the Watergate conspiracy convictions and the impeachment proceedings against President Nixon, it is that the separation of powers is the key to the viability of the American system of government—and to the protection of the liberty of all American citizens.

Nixon's Unconditional Pardon Ends New President's Political "Honeymoon"

President Ford's "honeymoon" period with Congress lasted exactly 30 days. It came to an abrupt end on September 8, 1974, when he unexpectedly granted former President Nixon an unconditional pardon for all federal crimes that he "committed or may have committed or taken part in" while in office. Capitol Hill reaction to President Ford's decision—reached without consulting his friends in Congress, his cabinet, or Leon Jaworski, the special Watergate prosecutor—was immediate and overwhelming. Democrats voiced pointed and detailed objections, raising questions of a dual standard of justice, the fairness of the pardon to other Watergate defendants, and whether the nation would ever know if Mr. Nixon was or was not guilty of the impeachment charges or possible conspiracy counts.

The unexpected, televised Sunday morning speech on executive clemency—made less than ten days after the new President had publicly announced that he would make no decision on a pardon until the "legal process" of the indictment and the trial had been completed—was especially damaging to Mr. Ford's credibility. At the stroke of a pen, President Ford had recklessly squandered his recently built public trust. Some commentators termed the pardon Mr. Ford's "Bay of Pigs"—an allusion to John F. Kennedy's ill-fated decision to support anti-Castro Cuban revolutionaries in 1961. In a special postpardon Gallup poll, commissioned by the *New York Times,* Mr. Ford's "approval" rating skidded from 71 percent to 49 percent over a three-week period.[7] Indeed, Mr. Ford was the first President since the founding of the Gallup organization in 1935 who failed to retain majority support of those polled during his first month in the White House. Most Republican lawmakers, however, temporarily supported the party line that President Ford had displayed compassion and tempered justice with mercy in granting former President Nixon an unconditional pardon in order to hasten healing the wounds of Watergate.

Congressional protests on both sides of the aisle, however, shot up several decibels two days later when the White House issued a report that President Ford was studying "the entire matter" of possible pardons for all Watergate defendants. Before the day was over, almost every member of Congress had expressed himself or herself as appalled at the thought of any blanket pardoning of the Watergate defendants. Within 24 hours, White House officials suddenly reversed their position and denied that blanket pardons were being considered. By this time the White House was in full retreat. Hundreds of telegrams and phone calls reached Capitol Hill. They ran 6 to 1 against the new President, almost approaching the torrent that followed the "Saturday night massacre" firing of Special Watergate Prosecutor Archibald Cox in October, 1973.

The swift congressional reaction to the presidential pardon signaled a return to partisan politics between the legislative and executive branches. Less than two days later, the Senate adopted by a vote of 55 to 24 a "Sense of the Senate" resolution urging the President to refrain from using his pardoning power for any Watergate defendants until the judicial process was completed in each case.[8] In the House Representative Bella Abzug (D.-N.Y.) and eight other representatives recognized that Nixon could not be "unpardoned." Nevertheless, they introduced a resolution calling on President Ford to answer a dozen pardon-related questions. Although the resolution was not expected to be approved, it pointed up questions that have been asked with rising frequency, including the following: What role did General Alexander M. Haig, Jr., the White House "chief of staff" under both Nixon and Ford, play in the pardon? Did President Ford have any certification from a physician or psychiatrist that the charges pending against Mr. Nixon were endangering his health? Was Mr. Nixon's resignation related in any way to a pardon?

Shortly thereafter, Senator Walter F. Mondale (DFL-Minn.) announced that he would propose a constitutional amendment allowing Congress to overrule a presidential pardon by a two-thirds vote of the House and Senate.[9] In a flurry of related activities on Capitol Hill, a house subcommittee slashed former President Nixon's expense allowances for his transition to private life from $850,000 to $398,000. Subsequently the House and Senate lowered the final figure to $200,000. This measure, which had been pushed by Mr. Ford's aides, faced rough sledding in both the House and Senate. The following week the same senate committee unanimously approved a bill which would prevent former President Nixon from taking custody of the Watergate tapes or destroying them.[10] In the closing days of the 93rd Congress the two houses passed a measure banning the transfer of the White House tapes to Mr. Nixon nullifying the agreement between President Ford and the former President.

In another round in the recent battle over senate insistence on exerting closer policy supervision over military aid abroad and foreign policy in general, the Senate voted overwhelmingly (62 to 16) in early October, 1974, to cut off military aid to Turkey —and then agreed to allow President Ford to suspend the ban until December 15, 1974. Though threatened with a presidential veto, the senate action put both houses of Congress on record for aid suspension to Turkey (considered the aggressor in the Cyprus military action) by majorities substantially more than the two-thirds required to override a veto.[11]

In a little-noticed but important action, during the same week the U.S. Senate also voted to terminate four national emergencies dating from the Great Depression and to curb the authority of the President to govern by emergency proclamation. By a unanimous voice vote and without debate, the Senate approved the National Emergencies Act that would end in one year the national emergencies proclaimed by President Franklin D. Roosevelt in 1933 during the Great Depression, by President Truman in 1950 to mobilize for the Korean War, and by President Nixon to deal with the threatened national postal strike in 1970 and an international monetary crisis in 1971.[12] The Senate Special Committee on Termination of the National Emergency discovered in late 1973 that none of the four proclamations contained any provision for ending a state of emergency. The bill was sent to the House where a similar measure, introduced by House Judiciary Committee Chairman Peter Rodino (D.-N.J.), is pending.

If passed by the House and signed by the President, the measure would suspend all but a handful of the more than 460 statutes that, if invoked by a presidential declaration of emergency, grant the chief executive virtually unchecked powers. This proposed National Emergencies Act, supported by President Ford, would also establish procedures under which Congress could terminate a future national emergency by concurrent resolution, which is not subject to a presidential veto. To avoid undue haste, however, the emergencies would not terminate until a year after enactment of the legislation to give the Administration and Congress time to devise substitutes for some emergency laws that are presently being used routinely by the federal government.

The National Emergencies Act would provide for a review every six months after an emergency has been proclaimed to decide if it should be terminated. Almost by accident, the senate study committee discovered that each of the last seven Presidents, if he had wished to use this broad authority, could have taken control of major private industries, censored news media, and imposed martial law in designated "military zones" that could, in theory, have covered the entire United States. In advocating the National Emergencies Act, cosponsor Senator Charles Mathias (R.-Md.) said that "permitting this body of potentially authoritarian power to continue in force in the absence of a valid national emergency poses a hazard to democratic government." [13] From a substantive view, this proposed curtailment of special national emergency legislation is unquestionably one of the most crucial measures recently pushed by the lawmakers to restore to Congress powers that its members have too easily —and sometimes casually—ceded to the White House over several decades.

Unmistakably, the mood has changed on Capitol Hill. When the Congress took its August, 1974, recess, Mr. Ford's popularity had been at a peak, and there was an almost universal era of good feeling. But when the lawmakers returned to Washington the day after the Nixon pardon, they discovered that the Watergate controversy had exploded all over again. The lawmakers blamed the new President's pardoning action for the revival of the Watergate issue. As for the swift change in presidential-congressional relations, the predominant feeling of most Washington observers was "that the change was deeper than the ending of a honeymoon." As members of the House and Senate lined up at the congressional broadcasting booth to tape messages for their constituents, their messages, according to a *New York Times* reporter, had a common theme: "The man who had been 'my good friend, Jerry Ford' was now just another President wielding arbitrary power, and some thought that that was the way it would continue to be." [14]

More than ever, members of the House and Senate seemed determined to use their rediscovered power to oversee presidential decision making and to exercise the necessary checks on the chief executive through the investigative power, control of the purse strings and, if needed, even the amendment process.

Clearly, in light of the "deroyalization" of the presidency, as evidenced by the congressional passage of the War Powers Act of 1973 and the Budget and Impoundment Control Act of 1974, the Senate Watergate investigation, the House Judiciary Committee's impeachment proceedings, the subsequent resignation of President Nixon, and the recent congressional "backlash" against President Ford's pardoning of former President Nixon, can there be serious doubt that a new power balance exists in the national capital as we move into the last quarter of the twentieth century?

FOOTNOTES

1. Mr. Nixon's second inauguration ceremony, which had just received heavy nationwide television coverage less than ten days earlier, may also have influenced him to avoid overexposure on television during this brief time span.
2. *Watergate: Its Implications for Responsible Government* (Washington, D.C.: National Academy of Public Administration, 1974), p. x. This report is summarized in the *Washington Post,* March 21, 1974.
3. *New York Times,* May 1, 1973.
4. *Ibid.,* August 21, 1973.
5. Dan Cordtz, "The Imperial Life Style of the US President," *Fortune,* vol. LXXXVIII (October, 1973), p. 144.
6. George E. Reedy, *The Twilight of the Presidency* (New York: World Publishing Co., 1970) p. 9.
7. Thomas E. Cronin, "The Textbook Presidency and Political Science," paper delivered at the 66th annual meeting of the American Political Science Association, Los Angeles, Calif., September 7–12, 1970, reprinted in *Congressional Record,* vol. 116 (October 5, 1970) pp. 34914–34928.
8. Robert Carr, Marver Bernstein, and Walter Murphy, *American Democracy in Theory and Practice,* 4th ed. (New York: Holt, Rinehart and Winston, 1965), p. 447.
9. William A. McClenaghan, *Magruder's American Government* (Boston: Allyn and Bacon, 1962), p. 262, as quoted by Thomas E. Cronin, *op. cit.,* p. 34927.
10. Arthur M. Schlesinger, Jr., *The Imperial Presidency* (Boston: Houghton-Mifflin, 1973).
11. *Ibid.,* p. 169.
12. *New York Times Magazine,* January 3, 1965, pp. 7, 42–46.
13. Schlesinger, *op. cit.,* p. 169.
14. *Ibid.,* p. 170.
15. *Ibid.*
16. Ronald C. Moe, ed., *Congress and the President* (Pacific Palisades, Calif: Goodyear Publishing Company, Inc., 1971), p. 3. See also David Halberstam, *The Best and the Brightest* (New York: Fawcett Crest, 1972).
17. *Ibid.*
18. Warren Weaver, Jr., *Both Your Houses* (New York: Praeger, 1972), pp. 280–286.
19. For an absorbing story of this journalistic "scoop," see Carl Bernstein and Bob Woodward, *All the President's Men* (New York: Simon and

Schuster, 1974). See also James McCartney, "The Washington *'Post'* and Watergate: How Two Davids Slew Goliath," *Columbia Journalism Review,* Vol. 12 (Summer 1973) pp. 8–22.
20. *Congressional Quarterly Weekly Report,* XXXI (Februry 10, 1973), p. 306.
21. For further details, see *New York Times,* July 13, 1974. The new law is also discussed in Chapter 6.

2

1. Edward S. Corwin, *The President: Office and Powers,* 4th ed. (New York: New York University Press, 1957), p. 307.
2. *Federalist,* No. 51.
3. *Two Treaties of Government* (Morley ed.) Chapter 11, p. 134 and Chapter 14, p. 159.
4. *Federalist,* No. 48.
5. Max Farrand, ed., *U.S. Constitutional Convention: Records of the Federal Convention* (New Haven: Yale Univ. Press, 1911).
6. For further discussion of the "checks and balances" and "separation of powers" doctrines, Pritchett, *The American Constitution,* 2nd ed. (New York: McGraw-Hill Book Company, 1968), pp. 9, 20, 174–177.
7. Cited in James MacGregor Burns, "The One Test for the Presidency," *New York Times Magazine,* May 1, 1960, p. 102.
8. A much more extensive treatment of this controversy can be examined in Edward S. Corwin, 4th ed. *The President: Office and Powers* (New York: New York University Press, 1957), pp. 86–87, 375. Chief Justice Taft in *Myers* v. *United States* 272, U.S. 52 (1926) also maintains this constitutional grant of power of removal to the President.
9. This exchange is to be found in several readers on the presidency. Excerpts from the exchange used above are found in Robert S. Hirschfield, ed., *The Power of the Presidency: Concepts and Controversy* (Chicago: Aldine Publishing Company, 1973), pp. 49–61.
10. Louis Koenig, *The Chief Executive* (New York: Harcourt, Brace and World, Inc., 1968 rev. ed., pp. 27–28.
11. Corwin, *op. cit.,* p. 17.
12. *Ibid.,* p. 18.
13. Wilfred E. Binkley, *President and Congress* (New York: Vintage Books, 1962 3rd rev. ed.), p. 67.
14. Koenig, *op. cit.,* p. 100.
15. Binkley, *op. cit.,* p. 75.
16. Edward S. Corwin, *op. cit.,* p. 21.
17. Binkley, *op cit.,* p. 110.
18. *Ibid.,* p. 154.
19. Cited in Clinton Rossiter, The American Presidency (New York: Mentor Books, 1960), p. 94.

20. Binkley, *op. cit.*, p. 138.
21. *Ibid.*, p. 142.
22. Cited in Binkley, *op. cit.*, p. 151.
23. Binkley, *op. cit.*, p. 457.
24. Irving Brant, *Impeachment Trials and Errors* (New York: Alfred A. Knopf, 1972), p. 138. For the full text of the articles of impreachment and the senate trial consult Richardson, *Messages and Papers of the President 1789–1897,* Vol. 6, pp. 709–725.
25. Woodrow Wilson, *Congressional Government* (1885) (New York: Meridian Edition, 1908), Vol. 1, p. 230.
26. James Bryce, *American Commonwealth* (New York: Commonwealth Edition, 1908), Vol. 1, p. 230.
27. Leonard D. White, *The Republican Era: 1869–1901* (New York: Macmillan Company, 1948), p. 113.
28. James MacGregor Burns, *Presidential Government: The Crucible of Leadership* (New York: Avon Books Edition, 1967), p. 65.
29. *Ibid.*, pp. 65–66.
30. *Ibid.*, pp. 69–70.
31. Leonard White, *op. cit.*, p. 109.
32. F. D. G. Riddle, *State and National Power Over Commerce* (New York: Columbia University Press, 1937), pp. 117–119.
33. Clinton Rossiter, *The American Presidency*, rev. ed. (New York: Mentor Books, 1962), p. 100.
34. Samuel E. Morison, *The Oxford History of the United States,* Vol. II (London: 1927), p. 449.
35. Binkley, *op. cit.*, p. 239.
36. Article III, Section 3.
37. Binkley, *op. cit.*, p. 260.
38. *Ibid.*, p. 281.
39. James David Barber, *The Presidential Character: Predicting Performance in the White House* (Englewood Cliffs, N.J.: Prentice-Hall, 1972), p. 233.
40. Cited in Binkley, *op. cit.*, p. 294.
41. Robert Sherrill, *Why They Call It Politics* (New York: Harcourt Brace and Jovanovich, 1972), p. 67.
42. E. Pendleton Herring, "The First Session of the Seventy-Third Congress," *American Political Science Review,* Vol. 2. (March, 1934), p. 7.
43. Corwin, *op. cit.*, pp. 285–287. For a table of presidential vetoes see Chapter 6.
44. William E. Leuchtenberg, *Franklin D. Roosevelt and the New Deal* (New York: Harper and Row, 1963), Chapter 14.
45. A fiscal year date is the year in which the budget expenditures are allocated. Fiscal year 1975 starts July 1, 1974 and runs until June 30, 1975. Figures cited are taken from the 1973 *World Almanac* (New

York: Newspaper Enterprise Association, Inc., 1972), p. 114. Under the Congressional Budget and Impoundment Control Act of 1974 the fiscal year will run from October 1 to September 30. Thus, the fiscal year 1977 will start October 1, 1976 and continue to September 30, 1977.
46. Domestic Council, Council on Environment Quality, Office of Consumer Affairs, Office of Science and Technology, Office of Telecommunications, Office of Intergovernmental Relations, Council of International Economic Policy, and the National Aeronautics and Space Council.
47. The *Christian Science Monitor,* December 6, 1972.
48. *Congressional Quarterly,* January 13, 1973, pp. 38–39. In addition, Louis Koenig in *The Chief Executive, op. cit.,* p. 155, notes that the President is the administrator for 7 percent of the nation's work force.

3

1. Henry Steele Commager, "The Presidency After Watergate," *New York Review of Books,* Vol. XX (October 18, 1973), p. 49.
2. Grant McConnell, *The Modern Presidency* (New York: St. Martin's Press, 1967, p. 35.
3. *Ibid.*
4. Clinton Rossiter, "President and Congress in the 1960's" in Marian D. Irish, ed., *Continuing Crisis in American Politics* (Englewood Cliffs, N.J.: Prentice-Hall, 1963), pp. 104–105.
5. *New York Times,* February 1, 1973.
6. William J. Keefe and Morris S. Ogul, *The American Legislative Process* (Englewood Cliffs, N.J.: Prentice-Hall, Inc., 1964), p. 30.
7. Ralph K. Huitt, "Congressional Organization in the Field of Money and Credit," in Commission on Money and Credit, *Fiscal and Debt Management Policies* (Englewood Cliffs, N.J.: Prentice Hall, 1963), p. 494, as quoted by David J. Vogler, *The Politics of Congress* (Boston: Allyn and Bacon, Inc., 1974), p. 15.
8. Woodrow Wilson, *Constitutional Government in the United States* (New York: Columbia University Press, 1908), p. 68.
9. Emmet John Hughes, *The Living Presidency* (New York: Coward, McCann and Geoghegan, Inc., 1972), p. 200.
10. Samuel P. Huntington, "Congressional Responses to the Twentieth Century," in David B. Truman, ed., *The Congress and America's Future* (New York: Columbia University Press, American Assembly, 1965), p. 30.
11. *Ibid.,* p. 23.
12. Alfred de Grazia, *Republic in Crisis: Congress Against the Executive Force* (New York: Federal Legal Publications, 1965), p. 7.

Footnotes

13. Wilfred Binkley, *President and Congress* (New York: Alfred A. Knopf, 1947), Chapters I–III.
14. John S. Saloma, III, *Congress and the New Politics* (Boston: Little, Brown and Company, 1969), p. 62.
15. *Ibid.*, p. 30.
16. Ronald C. Moe, ed., *Congress and the President* (Pacific Palisades, Calif.: Goodyear Publishing Company, 1971), p. 1.
17. Saloma, *op. cit.*, p. 35.
18. Thomas E. Cronin, "The Textbook Presidency and Political Science," paper delivered at the 66th annual meeting of the American Political Science Association, Los Angeles, September 7–12, 1970, reprinted in *Congressional Record,* Vol. 116 (October 5, 1970), pp. 34914–34928.
19. *Ibid.*
20. Moe, *op. cit.*, p. ix.
21. William Howard Taft, *Our Chief Magistrate and His Powers* (New York: Columbia University Press, 1916), p. 139.
22. As quoted by Louis W. Koenig, *The Chief Executive* (New York: Harcourt, Brace and World, Inc. 1964, p. 13.
23. John C. Livingston and Robert G. Thompson, *The Consent of the Governed,* 3rd. ed. (N.Y.: The Macmillan Company, 1971), p. 371.
24. *Theodore Roosevelt: An Autobiography* (New York: Scribner's, 1924), p. 357.
25. Quoted by Edward S. Corwin, *The President: Office and Powers,* 4th ed. (New York: New York University Press, 1954), p. 297.
26. *New York Times,* April 7, 1973.
27. Quoted in Donald Bruce Johnson and Jack L. Walker, eds., *The Dynamics of the American Presidency* (New York: John Wiley, 1964), pp. 134–135.
28. Quoted in Sidney Hyman, "What is the President's True Role?" *The New York Times Magazine,* September 7, 1958.
29. Richard Neustadt, *Presidential Power* (New York: John Wiley, 1960), pp. 9–10.
30. *Ibid.*, pp. 163–164.
31. Joseph E. Kallenbach, *The American Chief Executive* (New York: Harper and Row, 1966), p. 372.
32. As quoted in the *Saturday Evening Post,* March 21, 1964, by Robert H. Davidson, David M. Kovenock, and Michael K. O'Leary, *Congress in Crisis: Politics and Congressional Reform* (Belmont, Calif.: Wadsworth Publishing Company, 1966), p. 20.
33. Quoted in *New York Times,* April 28, 1974.
34. John Locke, *Second Treatise on Civil Government* (London: J. M. Dent & Sons, 1924), p. 190.
35. Louis Fisher, *President and Congress* (New York: The Free Press, 1972), p. 26.

36. *Federalist,* No. 48 (Oxford: Basil Blackwell, 1948), p. 253.
37. As quoted by Clinton Rossiter, *The American Presidency,* rev. ed. (New York: The American Library, 1960), p. 71.
38. *Federalist,* No. 48, *op. cit.,* p. 253.
39. Richard E. Neustadt, *op. cit.,* p. 33.
40. Warren Weaver, Jr., *Both Your Houses* (New York: Praeger, 1972), p. 275.
41. Aaron Wildavsky, "The Two Presidencies," *Transaction* (December, 1966), pp. 7–14 in Ronald Moe, ed., *Congress and the President, op. cit.,* p. 123.
42. Theodore H. White, *The Making of the President 1968* (New York: Atheneum, 1969), p. 147.
43. Cited in Aaron Wildavsky, "The Two Presidents," in Ronald Moe, *op. cit.,* p. 123.
44. James David Barber, *The Presidential Character* (Englewood Cliffs, N.J.: Prentice-Hall, Inc., 1972), p. 32.
45. Congressional Quarterly Service, *Congress and the Nation* 1945–64 (Washington, D.C., 1965). The 70 percent figure is from Wildavsky's "The Two Presidencies" in Moe, *op. cit.,* p. 122, and excludes legislation regarding refugees and immigration, largely considered by Congress as domestic policy.
46. Wildavsky's "The Two Presidencies," in Moe, *op. cit.,* p. 122.
47. As quoted in Robert Sherrill, *Why They Call It Politics* (New York: Harcourt, Brace, Jovanovich, 1972), p. 67.
48. Aaron Wildavsky, *op. cit.,* p. 242.
49. Ronald C. Moe and Steven C. Teel, "Congress as Policy-Maker: A Necessary Reappraisal," in Ronald C. Moe, ed., *Congress and the President* (Pacific Palisades, Calif.: Goodyear Publishing Company, Inc., 1971), p. 34.
50. *Ibid.,* p. 42.
51. *Ibid.*
52. Ralph K. Huitt, "Congress, the Durable Partner" in Ronald C. Moe, ed., *Congress and the President, op. cit.,* p. 298.
53. Rexford G. Tugwell and Thomas E. Cronin, *The Presidency Reappraised* (New York: Praeger, 1974), p. 7.

4

1. 299 U.S. 304 (1936).
2. Cited in Eleanor Lansing Dulles, *John Foster Dulles: The Last Year* (New York: Harcourt, Brace and World, 1963), p. 31.
3. J. William Fulbright, *The Crippled Giant: American Foreign Policy and its Domestic Consequences* (New York: Vintage Books, 1972), p. 228.

Footnotes

4. Edward S. Corwin, *The President—Office and Powers* (New York: New York University Press, 1957), 4th rev. ed., p. 171.
5. Woodrow Wilson, *Constitutional Government in the United States* (New York: Macmillan Publishing Co., 1908), p. 138.
6. *United States* v. *Curtiss-Wright Corporation,* 299 U.S. 304, 319 (1936).
7. Corwin, *op. cit.,* pp. 211–212.
8. *New York Times,* September 12, 1963.
9. W. S. Holt, *Treaties Defeated in the Senate* (Baltimore, 1933), 123, 165, is cited by Arthur M. Schlesinger, Jr., in *The Imperial Presidency* (Boston: Houghton Mifflin Co., 1973), p. 80.
10. Guy M. Gillette, "The Senate in Foreign Relations, *"Annals of the American Academy of Political and Social Science* 289 (September, 1953), 52–53, cited in an article by Cecil V. Crabb, Jr., entitled "The Role of Congress in Foreign Relations" in Ronald C. Moe's book *Congress and the President* (Pacific Palisades, Calif: Goodyear Publishing Company, Inc., 1971), p. 213.
11. Cited in Hans Morgenthau, "Congress and Foreign Policy," *The New Republic,* Vol. 160, (June 14, 1969), pp. 16–18.
12. Louis Fisher, *Congress and the President* (New York: The Free Press, 1972), p. 43.
12a. The United States Senate did ratify eight security treaties committing the United States to the defense of 43 nations during the height of the cold war era of the late 1940's and early 1950's.
13. Cited in Arthur M. Schlesinger, Jr., *op. cit.,* pp. 87–88.
14. *Ibid,* p. 104.
15. 301 U.S. 324, 330–31 (1937). This decision was reaffirmed six years later in *United States* v. *Pink* (1942).
16. Subcommittee on Separation of Powers, Senate Judiciary Committee, Congressional Oversight of Executive Agreements: Hearing, 92 Congress 2 Session (1972), p. 249.
17. C. F. Louis Henkin, *Foreign Affairs and the Constitution* (New York: Foundation Press, 1972), p. 420.
18. *United States* v. *Guy Capps, Inc.* (1953) 214 F2nd 655, 660.
19. *Seery* v. *United States* (1955) 127 F. Supp. 601, 606, and *Reid* v. *Covert,* 354 U.S. 1, 16 (1957).
20. Schlesinger, *op. cit.,* p. 313.
21. *Ibid.,* p. 313.
22. *Ibid.*
23. Symington Committee Reports in 12 volumes. Data taken from the volume on *Security Agreements* 91 Congress 2nd Session, December 21, 1970, p. 11–12.
24. J. William Fulbright, "Congress and Foreign Policy," in Ronald C. Moe, ed., *Congress and the President* (Pacific Palisades, Calif: Goodyear Publishing, 1971), pp. 197–209.

5

1. Irving L. Janis, *Victims of Groupthink* (Boston: Houghton Mifflin Co., 1972), p. 138.
2. Malcolm E. Jewell and Samuel C. Patterson, *The Legislative Powers in the United States* (New York: Random House, 1966), p. v.
3. For the Library of Congress compilation one can consult *Background Information on the Use of United States Armed Forces in Foreign Countries,* Committee print prepared for the House Committee on Foreign Affairs, 91st Congress, 2nd Session (1970), pp. 50–57.
4. From Meeker, "The Legality of United States Participation in the Defense of VietNam," 54 *Department of State Bulletin* (1966) 474, 484–485. The discrepancy between the 125 conflicts reported by the State Department in 1966 and the 165 conflicts reported by the Library of Congress in 1970 is in part accounted for by their definitions of military actions abroad as well as by institutional bias.
5. To examine the discussion of this question at the Constitutional Convention consult "Debates in the Federal Convention of 1787, as reported by James Madison, *Documents Illustrative of the Formation of the Union of the American States* (1927), pp. 561–563.
6. Cited in *Congressional Quarterly Guide to Current American Government,* 1968 (Washington, D.C.: Congressional Quarterly Service, 1969), pp. 61–64.
7. Rexford G. Tugwell, *The Enlargement of the Presidency* (Toronto: Doubleday Publishing Co., 1960), p. 124.
8. Cited in Robert Sherrill, *Why They Call It Politics* (New York: Harcourt, Brace and Jovanovich, Inc., 1972), p. 29.
9. *Public Papers of the President,* 1965, II, p. 616.
10. In James Grafton Rogers, *World Policing and the Constitution* (Boston: World Peace Foundation, 1945), p. 36. In the *Prize Cases,* 67 U.S. 635 (1863) the Supreme Court held that "if a war be made by invasion of a foreign nation, the President is not only authorized but is bound to accept the challenge without any legislative act."
11. Louis Fisher, *Congress and the President* (New York: The Free Press, 1972), p. 193. The Supreme Court permitted extension of wartime rent controls in the Housing and Rent Act of 1947 by recognizing in *Woods* v. *Miller,* 333 U.S. 138 (1948), the extended impact of war on the economy long after hostilities themselves have been concluded.
12. *Prize Cases,* 67 U.S. 635, (1863). On August 6, 1861, Congress declared by joint resolution that "all the acts, proclamations, and orders of the President—are hereby approved and in all respects made valid. . ." The Supreme Court did repudiate President Lincoln's suspension of a writ of habeas corpus in *Ex Parte Milligan,* 71 U.S. 22 (1866) *after*

the war on the grounds that civil courts, not military tribunals, should be used to try citizens when they are available.
13. Much of the historical material on expansion of presidential emergency power is cited in C. Q. *Guide to American Government* 1968 (Washington, D.C.: C. Q. Publication, 1968), pp. 61–64, and from Rexford G. Tugwell, *op. cit.*
14. 323 U.S. 214 (1944).
15. *Newsweek,* January 7, 1974, p. 15.
16. *Lansing State Journal* (Lansing, Michigan), "Congress Seeks to Blunt Presidential Power," March 20, 1974. If the President is so inclined, he presently has the authority to place almost any American in military detention; dispatch American forces to any nation he feels will assist in the interest of national defense; seize and control broadcasting and transportation industries; restrict travel; seize properties and commodities; and institute martial law, among a seemingly endless list of acts sanctioned by emergency legislation on the books. Also see Chapter 9.
17. James MacGregor Burns, "The Politics of the Presidency," in Ronald C. Moe, *Congress and the President: Allies and Adversaries* (Pacific Palisades, Calif: Goodyear Publishing Co., 1971), p. 291.
18. Samuel P. Huntington, "Strategic Planning and Political Process," *Foreign Affairs,* Vol. 38 (January, 1960), pp. 285, 291–292.
19. Cited in Richard Neustadt, *Presidential Power* (New York: The New American Library Edition, 1964), p. 50.
20. Patrick Anderson, *The President's Men* (New York: A Doubleday Book, 1969), p. 207.
21. Mr. Fitzgerald finally regained his job including all back pay, in 1973, after a three-year court battle. Fisher, *op. cit.,* p. 212.
22. Anderson, *op. cit.,* pp. 261, 323.
23. For a full text of the bill consult *New York Times,* November 8, 1973.
24. Cited in *Congressional Quarterly Guide,* (Washington, D.C.: Congressional Quarterly, 1973), p. 14.
25. Saul K. Padover, "The Power of the President," *Commonweal,* Vol. 88 (August 9, 1968), pp. 521–525.
26. John E. Mueller, *War, Presidents, and Public Opinion* (New York: John Wiley and Sons, Inc., 1973, pp. 15–16.
27. *New York Times,* November 18, 1973.

6

1. Richard Neustadt, *Presidential Power* (New York: John Wiley & Sons, 1960), p. 53.
2. Dennis J. Polumbo, *American Politics* (New York: Appleton Century Crofts, 1973), p. 252. The Nixon quote is from Rowland Evans, Jr., and

R. D. Novak, *Nixon and the White House: The Frustration of Power* (New York: Random House, 1971), p. 107.

3. Reorganization within the executive branch takes effect 60 days after the President issues an executive order unless voted down by a concurrent resolution of both houses of Congress.
4. John M. Pfiffner and Robert Presthus, *Public Administration,* 5th ed. (New York: The Ronald Press, 1967), p. 5, and Samuel P. Huntington, "Congressional Responses to the Twentieth Century" in *The Congress and America's Future,* David B. Truman, ed. (Englewood Cliffs, N.J.: Prentice-Hall, 1965), p. 23.
5. Louis Fisher, *President and Congress: Power and Policy* (New York: The Free Press, 1972), p. 105.
6. Richard E. Neustadt, "Presidency and Legislation: Planning the President's Program" cited in Aaron Wildavsky, *The Presidency* (Boston: Little Brown & Company, 1969), p. 595.
7. *Ibid.,* p. 594. The absence of an Eisenhower attitude on form and character of legislation in the foreign aid program was the catalyst for the remark.
8. Aaron Wildavsky, *The Politics of the Budgetary Process* (Boston: Little Brown and Company, 1964), pp. 1–3.
9. *Christian Science Monitor,* September 11, 1973. The White House and the Capitol are located on either end of Pennsylvania Avenue.
10. Willmoore Kendall, "The Two Majorities" from Ronald C. Moe, ed., *Congress and The President* (Pacific Palisades, Calif: Goodyear Publishing Company, 1971), p. 271.
11. Patrick Anderson, The President's Men (New York: Doubleday and Company, Inc., 1969), pp. 295–312.
12. Congressional Quarterly Service, *Legislators and the Lobbyists,* 2nd ed., May 1968 (Washington, D.C.: Congressional Quarterly, Inc., 1968), p. 65.
13. *Ibid.,* p. 68.
14. Footnote material in parentheses.
15. Common Cause, *Report from Washington,* Vol. 3, Number 4, March 1973, p. 4 shows that the caucus vote on House Committee chairmen has been overwhelming for the senior majority member of each committee.
16. Bicameralism refers to a two-house legislative body.
17. Bruce R. Hopkins, *American Bar Association Journal,* Vol. 59 (February 1973), pp. 147–148.
18. *New York Times,* July 13, 1974.
19. *Washington Post,* March 22, 1974.
20. Fisher, *op. cit.,* pp. 25, 47, and 48.
21. *Ibid.,* p. 155–170.

Footnotes

22. Bruce Hopkins, *op. cit.,* pp. 146–149.
23. *New York Times,* July 26, 1973.
24. *Ibid.*
25. *Ibid.*
26. *New York Times,* September 21, 1974.
27. *New York Times,* March 13, 1973.
28. Excerpts from oral arguments by Special Watergate Prosecutor Leon Jaworski and the President's lawyer, Mr. James St. Clair, before the U.S. Supreme Court, *New York Times,* July 9, 1974.
29. *Ibid.*
30. Text of Supreme Court ruling ordering Nixon to turn over data, *New York Times,* July 25, 1974.
31. *Ibid.,* and *Marbury* v. *Madison,* 1 Cranch 137 (1803).
32. *Ibid.*
33. The Dixon-Yates controversy formed another chapter in the continuing struggle between TVA and private power companies over public versus private ownership of electric power facilities in the South.
34. *New York Times,* June 14, 1973.
35. Woodrow Wilson, *Congressional Government* (Boston: Houghton Mifflin Company, 1885), p. 303.
36. *Barenblatt* v. *United States,* 360 U.S. 109 (1959).
37. Fisher, *op. cit.,* pp. 81–85. This is an excellent source for legislative oversight and presentation of the legislative veto and its use.

7

1. Nelson Polsby, *Congress and the Presidency,* 2nd ed. (Englewood Cliffs, N.J.: Prentice-Hall, 1971), p. 171.
2. Richard Neustadt, *Presidential Power* (New York: John Wiley, 1960), p. 37.
3. Reported in *Congressional Quarterly Almanac* for 1953 by Louis Koenig, *The Chief Executive* (New York: Harcourt, Brace and Jovanovich, 1968), p. 146.
4. Julius Turner, *Party and Constituency: Pressures on Congress* (Baltimore: Johns Hopkins, 1951), Lewis A. Froman, Jr. *Congressmen and Their Constituencies* (Chicago: Rand McNally, 1963), pp. 88–89.
5. Nelson Polsby, *op. cit.,* p. 146.
6. A discussion of this act and background leading to its passage will be found in Chapter 5.
7. Edward S. Corwin, *The President: Office and Powers,* 4th ed. (New York: New York University Press, 1957), pp. 297–299.
8. Charles S. Hyneman, *Bureaucracy in a Democracy* (New York: Harper & Row, 1950), p. 25.

9. Joseph E. Kallenbach, *The American Chief Executive* (New York: Harper & Row, 1966), p. 575.
10. Herman Finer, *The Presidency: Crisis and Regeneration* (Chicago: University of Chicago Press, 1950), Chapter VII.
11. H. J. Res 903 (93rd Congress, 2nd Session) February 14, 1974, copy supplied by Representative Reuss. For a more detailed discussion of the Reuss plan, see Henry S. Reuss, "A No-Confidence Amendment," *Commonweal,* Vol. C (April 12, 1974), pp. 127–129.
12. James L. Sundquist, "Needed: A Workable Check on the President" *The Brookings Bulletin,* Vol. 10 (Fall 1973), p. 11.
13. *Ibid.*
14. *Ibid.*
15. *Ibid.*
16. Charles M. Hardin, *Presidential Power and Accountability Toward a New Constitution* (Chicago: University of Chicago Press, 1974).
17. *Ibid.,* p. 183.
18. Rowland Egger, *The President of the United States* (New York: McGraw-Hill Book Company, 1967), p. 157.
19. *Ibid.*
20. *Ibid.,* pp. 151–152.
21. In this section we have relied heavily on Thomas E. Cronin, "The Swelling of the Presidency and Its Impact on Congress," *Working Papers on House Committee Organization and Operation,* Select Committee on Committees (Washington, D.C.: Government Printing Office), June 1973, p. 17.
22. *Ibid.,* p. 17.
23. "Restoring the Federal Balance," *Time,* Vol. 103 (May 6, 1974), p. 14.
24. T. E. Cronin, *op. cit.,* p. 16.
25. Richard N. Goodwin, "Dismantling the Presidency: Advise, Consent, and Restrain," *Rolling Stone,* March 14, 1974.
26. T. E. Cronin, *op. cit.,* p. 16.
27. President Ford's thinking, as reported by some of his associates shortly before his congressional appearance, was "that executive privilege is a valid concept but that some of the old postures do not always work in the temper of the times." Mr. Ford's flexible view on executive privilege may have stemmed from his earlier experience in the House of Representatives. In the early 1960's Mr. Ford was highly critical of the Kennedy Administration when General Maxwell Taylor, at that time chairman of the Joint Chiefs of Staff, refused to answer questions posed by a defense subcommittee on appropriations for the Bay of Pigs operation. *New York Times,* October 1, 1974.
28. "Restoring the Federal Balance," *op. cit.,* p. 14.
29. *New York Times,* November 14, 1973. Ironically, President Nixon

introduced a bill similar to the Hart-Bayh independent prosecutor proposal when he was a member of the U.S. Senate in 1951! *Ibid.,* November 2, 1973.
30. Thomas E. Cronin, *op. cit.,* p. 17.

8

1. *New York Times,* November 18, 1973.
2. *Ibid.,* July 26, 1974.
3. *Ibid.,* February 5, 1974.
4. *Ibid.,* June 16, 1974.
5. *Ibid.,* October 9, 1973.
6. *Ibid.*
7. *Washington Post,* July 13, 1974.
8. "Bold Reforms for Better Budgeting," *Time,* Vol. 103 (April 1, 1974), p. 17.
9. Attorney General Richard Kleindienst, John Mitchell's successor, testifying before a senate subcommittee in April, 1973, echoed the "Gerry Ford" theory. As Kleindienst put it, "You do not need facts to impeach the President . . . you do not need evidence." All that is required, he said, is votes. Both the Ford and Kleindienst statements are included in a summary of a Justice Department report on impeachment, compiled by the Department's Office of Legal Counsel and summarized in the *Washington Post,* February 28, 1974.
10. *Washington Post,* March 16, 1974.
11. Raoul Berger, *Impeachment: The Constitutional Problems* (Cambridge, Mass.: Harvard University Press, 1973), p. 122.
12. *Ibid.,* p. 98.
13. Raoul Berger, Impeachment, An Instrument of Regeneration, *Harpers,* Vol. 248 (January, 1974), p. 14.
14. Raoul Berger, "Impeachment for High Crimes and Misdemeanors," Southern California Law Review, 395 (1971), as quoted in *Impeachment, Committee of the Judiciary,* 93rd Congress, 1st Session (Washington, D.C.: Government Printing Office, 1973), p. 658.
15. *New York Times,* February 22, 1974.
16. *Ibid.*
17. *The Law of Presidential Impeachment,* (New York: Association of the Bar of the City of New York, January 1974), p. 8.
18. *Ibid.*
19. *New York Times,* March 1, 1974.
20. *Ibid.*
21. *Ibid.*
22. *Washington Post,* February 28, 1974.

23. *New York Times,* February 7, 1974.
24. *Congressional Quarterly Weekly Report,* XXXII (February 2, 1974), p. 230.
25. The term "executive privilege" has been discussed in Chapter 6.
26. *New York Times,* July 25, 1974.
27. *Ibid.*
28. *Ibid.,* August 1, 1974.
29. *Washington Post,* August 1, 1974.
30. *New York Times,* August 4, 1974.
31. *Washington Post,* August 1, 1974.
32. *Detroit Free Press,* August 3, 1974.
33. *Ibid.*
34. Louis Koenig, *The Chief Executive* (New York: Harcourt, Brace and World, Inc., 1965), p. 67.
35. *New York Times,* March 18, 1974.
36. *Ibid.,* August 4, 1974.
37. *Ibid.*
38. *Detroit Free Press,* August 4, 1974.

9

1. Arthur Schlesinger, Jr., *The Imperial Presidency* (Boston: Houghton Mifflin, 1973), pp. 312–315.
2. *New York Times,* May 24, 1973.
3. Associated Press, Correspondent Walter R. Mears, *Lansing* (Michigan) *State Journal,* December 13, 1973.
4. *Ibid.*
5. See Summary of *Emergency Power Statutes,* Special Committee on the Termination of the National Emergency, United States Senate, (Washington, D.C.: U.S. Government Printing Office, October 1973), pp. 1–74.
6. *Detroit Pree Press,* July 28, 1974.
7. *New York Times,* September 12, 1974.
8. *Ibid.,* September 13, 1974.
9. *Seattle Post-Intelligencer,* September 11, 1974.
10. The Senate, by a vote of 56 to 7, approved in early October, 1974, the measure to cancel the arrangement that gave former President Nixon custody of his White House tapes and papers. Senior Republicans attacked the bill as an unconstitutional, emotional reaction to Watergate. But even Senate Republican Leader Hugh Scott and his assistant, Robert P. Griffin, voted for the measure after attempts to delay or dilute it failed, by margins of 3 to 1. New York Times, October 5, 1974.
11. *Seattle Post-Intelligencer,* October 10, 1974.

Footnotes

12. *New York Times,* October 8, 1974.
13. Senator Charles Mathias (R.-Md.), one of the cosponsors, said that before he and Senator Frank Church (D.-Ida.) introduced the bill in late August, 1974, they met with President Ford and agreed "to work with the executive branch at every stage and to consider any new proposals that might be made." *Ibid.*
14. John Herbers, New York Times, September 15, 1974.

TOPICS FOR PAPER OR ORAL ★ REPORTS based on material and bibliography in the Politics of Government Series

1. Action and Interaction of Interest Groups upon Each Other
2. The Impact of Interest Groups upon Public Opinion
3. The Influence of Invisible Government
4. Means of Communications and Public Opinion
5. Responsibility of Lobbyists
6. Effective Techniques of Lobbyists
7. Advantages of the National Party Convention
8. Influence of Martin Van Buren on the National Nominating Process
9. Success of the National Nominating Conventions
10. Purpose of the National Party Convention
11. Early Experiments in the National Nominating Process
12. Andrew Jackson and the Nominating Process
13. Proposals for Breaking up the Ghettos
14. The Vast Problems of the Central Cities
15. The Feeling of "Anomie" and its Cause
16. The Influence of 19th Century Immigrants on Municipal Government
17. Problems Created by Ethnics and Blacks in the Inner City
18. Home Rule for Large Cities
19. The Effect of Unionization of City Employees on Local Government
20. Responsiblility of State Government for the Cities
21. Fiscal Responsibility of State Governments
22. Advantages of the Corporation
23. The Importance of Bigness in Corporate Enterprise
24. The Meaning of Laissez Faire
25. Significance of the Industrial Revolution
26. The Doctrine of Social Responsibility
27. The Split Atom of Property
28. The Policy of Competition
29. Recognition of the Rights of the Consumer
30. The Making of a Successful Lobbyist

Topics for Papers or Oral Reports

31 Effectiveness of the Business Lobby
32 Labor as an Interest Group
33 Legislative Work of the League of Women Voters
34 New York City as Lobbyist
35 Public Interest Lobbies
36 The Success of Lobbies
37 The Political Process of Government
38 The Power of Occupational Interest Groups
39 The Protection of People in the Cross-fire of Lobbies
40 Proposals for Change of the Welfare System
41 Factors that Contribute to Slum Conditions
42 Changing Economic Life Within the Cities
43 The Problems of Urban Renewals
44 The Conflict of so many Federal Grants
45 Sources of State Revenue
46 Limitation of the Taxing Power of the City
47 Government Regulation of Business
48 Welfare Government
49 The New Deal and Business
50 The War Economy
51 The Anti-Establishment Movement
52 The Beginning of the Party System
53 Masonic Influence in New York
54 The Era of Personal Politics and its Collapse
55 The Emerging Democratic Party 1824–1836
56 The Early Democratic Party in New York State
57 Significance of the Presidential Primaries
58 The McGovern Commission Report on Reforms
59 The Making of the Party Platform
60 The Rights of Stockholders
61 The Demands of Labor
62 New Responsibilities of Business
63 Corporations and Pollution
64 The Problem of the Automobile
65 Business and the Oil Spillage
66 The Formation of Public Policy
67 The Weakness of Interest Groups
68 Functional Representation v. Geographical Representation
69 Proposed Reforms for Lobbying
70 Financial Crises of the Cities
71 Confusion Arising from many Special Governmental Districts
72 The Relations of the Federal Grant-in-Aid System and Levels of Government
73 The Quality of Life in the Big Cities

74 The Model Cities Program
75 Civil Rights and Economic Opportunity
76 The Corporations and the Disadvantaged
77 Recommendations of the Advisory Commission on Intergovernmental Relations
78 Limitation upon the Taxing Power of the City
79 The New Relation of the County and the City
80 The Confusion of Many Planning Boards
81 The Different Forms of Municipal Government
82 Recent Reforms in Big City Administrations
83 Comparison of Controls Exercised by State and Urban Governments
84 Educational Inadequacies of Minority-group Children
85 The National Environmental Policy Act (1963)
86 The Future of the Corporations
87 Proposals for Replacement of the National Nominating Conventions
88 Early Planning for a National Party Convention
89 The Work of the Four Major Committees of the National Party Convention
90 Choosing Delegates to the National Party Convention
91 Control of the National Party Convention
92 The Floor Organization at the National Party Convention
93 Presidential Availability
94 Major Attacks upon the Convention System
95 Why the "Head-start" Program Failed
96 Proposals to Increase Participation of the People
97 The Problem of School Decentralization
98 Future Plans for Welfare
99 The Place of the Cities in the Federal System
100 Proposals for Change in the Big Cities
101 Origin of the National Commission on Civil Disorders
102 Reasons for Black Separatism
103 Effectiveness of Community Action Programs
104 Accomplishments of the War on Poverty Program
105 Megalopolis Viewed as a New Level of Government
106 The Problems of Pluralism
107 Weakness Inherent in Local Participation
108 Need for Assimilation in the Big Cities
109 Rigidity of Ethnic Cohesion
110 Black Problems in the Ghetto
111 Achievements of the Model City Programs
112 Urban Decentralization
113 The New York City Experiment with School Decentralization
114 Functioning of the Neighborhood Development Corporations
115 Revival of the Old Town Meeting

Topics for Papers or Oral Reports

116 Learning Progress in the Integrated Schools
117 Participation versus Efficiency in Government
118 Drafting a Bill for the State Legislature
119 Decentralizing the School Board in New York City
120 Procedure for Lobbying
121 Distinguish between Local Control and Local Participation
122 The Police and Community Co-operation
123 Community Conference Planning
124 Volunteer Assistants for the Fire Department
125 Black Power—In the Ghetto? In Business? In Politics?
126 Causes of Alienation
127 The Ways to End Alienation
128 The Making of a Law
129 Responsibility of the Voter
130 The State and the People: Rule and Regulations
131 The Importance of the Primary Election
132 Significance of Party Leadership in the Legislature
133 Impact of One-Man-One-Vote Mandate
134 Effectiveness of the Gerrymander
135 Powers of the Speaker in Legislative Matters
136 Purpose of the Party Caucus in the Legislature
137 Manipulation of the Legislators
138 Influence of Important Lobbyists
139 Limitations Caused by Rigid Procedure
140 Function of the Committee System in the Legislature
141 A Bill Becomes a Law
142 Responsibility of Budget Making in the Legislature
143 The Governor's Prerogatives Over the Legislature
144 The Power of Patronage
145 Separation of Powers in State Government
146 The Influence of Lobbying
147 Weakness of Registration
148 Needed Reforms of the Legislature
149 Staffing the Committees
150 Committee Hearings
151 The Citizen and the Legislature
152 Power of the Committee Chairman in Congress
153 Power of the Committee Chairman in the Legislature
154 Influence of Labor Unions on Legislation
155 The Government Lobby—Why?
156 Expanded Meaning of the First Amendment
157 Is there a Need for the Public Lobby—Common Cause?
158 Comparison of Private Lobbies with Public Lobbies
159 Comparison of successful and Unsuccessful Lobbying Practices

160 The Abuse of Lobbying
161 Needed Rules and Regulations for Lobbying
162 Method of the New Co-operative Lobbying
163 The Apportionment Rule of the 1972 Democratic Convention
164 Comparison of the Democratic Conventions of 1968 and 1972
165 Reasons for the poor Image of the Democratic Convention 1972 before the Public
166 How McGovern Lost the Election at the Miami Convention
167 How the 1972 Convention Split the Democratic Party
168 The Dramatic Rise of George Wallace as a Presidential Candidate 1972
169 Making of the New Majority 1972
170 The Conservative Sweep in the Election of 1972
171 The South Gets Reconverted 1972
172 The Ingredients for Getting Elected in a National Presidential Campaign
173 Graft in Politics
174 Graft in Office
175 Can the Citizen be Heard
176 Growth of Presidential Powers
177 The Presidency Acquires Majesty
178 The Disillusionment of Grandeur
179 The Sovereign Powers of Congress
180 The Real Meaning of Watergate
181 The Development of Executive Privilege
182 Influence of John Locke on the American Constitution
183 The Balanced Constitution
184 The Opposition to Andrew Jackson
185 The Whig Party—The Party of Congress
186 The Un-Constitutional Powers of Abraham Lincoln
187 The Rules for Impeachment, *1868, 1974*
188 Impact of Teddy Roosevelt on the Presidency
189 Comparison of the "Question Hour" in British Parliament with the Press Conference in America
190 The Maneuvering of Congress by FDR
191 The Presidency Becomes Institutionalized
192 Congressional Leadership
193 Executive Powers
194 The Treaty-making Procedure
195 Executive Agreements
196 The Powers of the Commander-in-Chief
197 Restraint of Congress—"All Legislative Powers Herein Granted."
198 Effective Use of Veto Power
199 Importance of Presidential Messages to Congress

Topics for Papers or Oral Reports

200 The Power of Committee Chairmen
201 The Meaning of "Oversight."
202 Purpose of Investigations
203 Significance of Party Discipline
204 Development of Bi-Partisan Foreign Policy
205 Co-operation between the President and Congress
206 Proposed Reforms of President-Congress Relations
207 Decline of the Presidency
208 Reforms of Congress
209 Powers of Judiciary Committee
210 Confidentiality and Its Implications

BIBLIOGRAPHY ★

Books

Anderson, Patrick, *The President's Men.* New York: Doubleday, 1969.

Barber, James David, *The Presidential Character.* Englewood Cliffs, New Jersey: Prentice Hall, 1972.

Berger, Raoul, *Executive Privilege.* Cambridge, Mass: Harvard University Press, 1974.

―――――, *Impeachment: The Constitutional Problems.* Cambridge Mass: Harvard University Press, 1973.

Bernstein, Carl and Woodward, Bob, *All the President's Men.* New York: Simon and Schuster, 1974.

Binkley, Wilford E., *President and Congress.* 3rd ed. New York: Vintage Books, 1962.

Black, Charles L., Jr., *Impeachment: A Handbook.* New Haven, Conn: Yale University Press, 1974.

Brant, Irving, *Impeachment Trials and Errors.* New York: Alfred A. Knopf, 1972.

Bryce, James, *American Commonwealth.* 3 vols., New York: The MacMillan Company, 1888.

Burnham, James, *Congress and the American Tradition.* Chicago: Henry Regnery, 1959.

Burns, James MacGregor, *Presidential Government: The Crucible of Leadership.* Boston: Houghton Mifflin, 1973.

Chamberlain, Lawrence H., *The President Congress and Legislation.* New York; Columbia University Press, 1946.

Corwin, Edward S., *The President: Office and Powers.* 4th ed., New York: New York University Press, 1957.

Davidson, Roger H., Kovenock, David M., and O'Leary, Michael K., *Congress in Crisis: Politics and Congressional Reform.* Belmont, California: Wadsworth Publishing Company, 1966.

DeGrazia, Alfred, *Republic in Crisis: Congress Against the Executive Force.* New York: Federal Legal Publications, 1965.

―――――, ed., *Congress: The First Branch of Government.* Washington, D.C.: American Enterprise Institute, 1966.

Bibliography

Egger, Rowland, *The President of the United States*. New York: McGraw Hill, 1967.

Evans, Rowland, Jr., and Novak, Robert. *Nixon and the White House: The Frustration of Power*. New York: Random House, 1971.

Finer, Herman, *The Presidency: Crisis and Regeneration*. Chicago, University of Chicago Press, 1960.

Fisher, Louis, *President and Congress*. New York: The Free Press, 1972.

Froman, Louis A., Jr., *Congressmen and Their Constituencies*. Chicago: Rand McNally, 1963.

Fulbright, J. William, *The Crippled Giant: American Foreign Policy and Its Domestic Consequences*. New York: Vintage Books, 1972.

Hardin, Charles M., *Presidential Power and Accountability: Toward a New Constitution*. Chicago: University of Chicago Press, 1974.

Hirschfield, Robert S., (ed.), *The Power of the Presidency: Concepts and Controversy*. 2nd ed., Chicago: Aldine, 1973.

Holtzman, Abraham, *Legislative Liaison: Executive Leadership in Congress*. Chicago, Rand McNally, 1970.

Hughes, Emmet John, *The Living Presidency*. New York: Coward, McCann and Geohagen, Inc., 1972.

Hyman, Sidney, *The American President*. New York: Harper and Brothers, 1954.

Johnson, Donald Bruce, and Walker, Jack L. (eds.), *The Dynamics of American Presidency*. New York: John Wiley, 1964.

Kallenbach, Joseph E., *The American Chief Executive*. New York: Harper and Row, 1966.

Koenig, Louis, *The Chief Executive*. New York: Harcourt, Brace and World, Inc., rev. ed., 1968.

Laski, Harold, *The American Presidency*. New York: Harper Row, 1940.

McConnell, Grant, *The Modern Presidency*. New York: St. Martin's Press, 1967.

Moe, Ronald C., (ed.), *Congress and the President*. Pacific Palesades, California: Goodyear Publishing Company, Inc. 1971.

Muller, John E., *War, Presidents and Public Opinion*. New York: John Wiley and Sons, Inc., 1973.

Neustadt, Richard, *Presidential Power*. New York: John Wiley and Sons, 1960.

Polsby, Nelson, *Congress and the Presidency*. 2nd ed., Englewood Cliffs, New Jersey, Prentice-Hall, 1971.

Reedy, George E., *The Twilight of the Presidency*. New York: World Publishing Co., 1970.

Rossiter, Clinton, *The American Presidency*. New York: Mentor Books, 1960.

Saloma, John S. III, *Congress and the New Politics*. Boston: Little, Brown and Company, 1969.

Schlesinger, Arthur, M., Jr., *The Imperial Presidency.* Boston: Houghton Mifflin, Co., 1973.

Schlesinger, Arthur, M., Jr., and DeGrazia, Alfred, *Congress and the Presidency: Their Role in Modern Times.* Washington, D.C.: American Enterprise Institute, 1967.

Sherrill, Robert, *Why They Call It Politics.* New York, Harcourt, Brace, and Jovanovich, 1972.

Taft, William Howard, *Our Chief Magistrate and His Powers.* New York: Columbia University Press, 1916.

Truman, David B., (ed.), *The Congress and America's Future.* New York: Columbia University, American Assembly, 1965.

Tugwell, Rexford G., *The Enlargement of the Presidency.* Toronto: Doubleday, 1960.

_____, and Cronin, Thomas E., *The Presidency Reappraised.* New York: Praeger, 1974.

Weaver, Warren, Jr., *Both Your Houses.* New York: Praeger, 1972.

White, Theodore, *The Making of A President, 1968.* New York: Atheneum, 1969.

Wilson, Woodrow, *Congressional Government.* Boston: Houghton-Mifflin, 1885.

Articles

Berger, Raoul, "Impeachment: An Instrument of Regeneration," *Harper's,* Vol. 248 (Jan., 1974), pp. 14–22.

"Bold Reforms for Better Budgeting," *Time,* Vol. 103 (April 1, 1974), pp. 17–18.

Commager, Henry S., "The Presidency After Watergate," *New York Review of Books,* Vol. XX (Oct. 18, 1974), pp. 49–53.

Cordtz, Dan, "The Imperial Life Style of the U.S. President," *Fortune,* Vol. LXXXVIII, (October, 1973), pp. 143–147.

Cronin, Thomas E., "The Swelling of the Presidency," *Saturday Review of the Society,* Vol. 1, (Feb. 1973), pp. 30–36.

_____, "Making the Presidency Safe for Democracy," *The Center Magazine,* Center for the Study of Democratic Institutions, Santa Barbara, California, Vol. VI, (Sept.–Oct., 1973), pp. 25–31.

_____, "The Textbook Presidency and Political Science," reprinted in *Congressional Record,* Vol. 116 (Oct. 5, 1970), pp. 34914–34928.

Goodwin, Richard N., "Dismantling the Presidency Advise Consent and Restrain, *Rolling Stone,* March 14, 1974, pp. 13–15.

Hyman, Sidney, "What is the President's True Role?" *New York Times Magazine,* Sept. 7, 1958.

McCartney, James, "The *Washington Post* and Watergate: How Two

Davids Slew Goliath," *Columbia Journalism Review,* Vol. 12 (Summer 1973), pp. 8–22.

Neustadt, Richard E., "The Constraining of the President," *New York Times Magazine* (Oct. 14, 1973), pp. 38–39, 110.

Padover, Saul, "The Power of the President," *Commomweal,* Vol. 88, (Aug. 9, 1968), pp. 521–525.

Schlesinger, Arthur M., Jr., "The Runaway Presidency," *The Atlantic Monthly,* Vol. 232 (Nov. 1973), pp. 43–55.

Sundquist, James L., "Needed: A Workable Check on the Presidency," *The Brookings Bulletin,* Vol. 10 (Fall 1973), pp. 7–11.

Wildavsky, Aaron, "The Two Presidencies," *Transaction,* Vol. 4 (December 1966), pp. 7–14.

INDEX ★

Adams, President John   19, 20, 71
Adams, Sherman   37
Albert, Speaker Carl   114, 128, 157, 161–162
Alien and Sedition Acts   20
Anderson, Senator Clinton   118, 128
Anderson, Rep. John B.   161
Appointment, Presidential   118–120, 143
Arthur, President Chester A.   27
Articles of Confederation   57, 70
Atomic Energy Act   64–65

Bayh, Senator Birch   145
Beard, Charles   40
Berger, Raoul   152–153
Bicameralism   108
Bricker Amendment   76, 79
Brooke, Senator Edward   162
Buchanan, President James   23, 47–48
Buchanan, Patrick J.   160
Budget and Accounting Act of 1921   29, 102, 109, 115
Budget and Impoundment Control Act of 1974   12, 55–56, 109–111, 150 165, 174
Burger, Chief Justice Warren   117
Burns, James MacGregor   89
Butler, Pierce   18–19, 83

Calhoun, Senator John C.   21, 39
Cambodia, U.S. bombing of   3, 12, 55, 149, 166
Cannon, Speaker Joseph "Uncle Joe"   30–31, 39
Carswell, G. Harrold   119
Case, Senator Clifford   79–80, 85, 91, 93, 166
Central Intelligence Agency   11, 85, 90
Chamberlain, Lawrence   64
Checks and balances   8, 15, 18, 65–66
Church, Senator Frank   88, 168
Civil War   22
Clay, Henry   21, 39
Cleveland, President Grover   27
Commager, Henry Steele   40
Congressionalists   42–43
Congressional Research Service   108, 115
Constitution, U.S.   16–18, 44, 58;   Foreign Affairs   67, 69;   War Makin 81–83;   Legislative Powers   96–97
Coolidge, President Calvin   121

Index

Corwin, Edward S. 16, 68, 71, 133, 140–141
Council of Economic Advisors 37
Council on Environmental Quality 37
Cox, Archibald (Special Watergate Prosecutor) 13, 119, 128, 145, 156, 171
Cronin, Thomas ix, 46, 143
Cuban Missile Crisis 63, 81, 91, 94, 128
Curtis, Rep. Thomas B. 106, 107

Dean, John W. III 147
Depression, Great 6, 32–33, 36, 50, 170
Dirksen, Senator Everett M. 7, 72, 127
Domestic Council 37
Drinan, Father Robert F. 157
Dulles, Sec. of State John Foster 74, 76

Eagleton, Senator Thomas 166
Eastern Establishment 7
Ehrlichman, John 2, 3
Eisenhower, President Dwight David 1, 37, 51, 53, 59, 74, 85, 126;
  Eisenhower Doctrine 60
Ellsberg, Daniel 120, 151
Emancipation Proclamation 24
Ervin, Senator Sam 11, 79–80, 93, 111
Executive Agreements 49, 75–79; Executive Agreements Act 1972 92
Executive dominance theory 43
Executive Office of President 36–37, 102, 142
executive orders 112
executive privilege viii, 14, 20, 113–115, 139, 140, 142, 153
Executive Reorganization Act of 1939 102

Federal Bureau of Investigation 11, 14
Federalist Papers 18, 57, 70
filibuster 108
Findley, Rep. Paul 161
Finer, Herman 135
Fireside chats 35, 50
Fitzgerald, A. E. 90
Ford, President Gerald 114–115, 144–145, 152, 162, 164; Nixon pardon 170–174
foreign affairs 67–80
Frey, Rep. Louis 160
Fulbright, Senator J. William 67, 80, 122, 162

General Accounting Office 44, 143
Gillette, Senator Guy 74

Goldwater, Senator Barry M. 7, 130
Goldwater, Rep. Barry M., Jr. 168
Goodwin, Richard V. 144
Gray, L. Patrick III 119, 147
Griffin, Senator Robert F. 14
Gulf of Tonkin Resolution see Vietnam War

Haldeman, H. R. 2
Hamilton, Alexander 19–20, 40, 85
Hardin Plan 134, 137–139
Harlow, Bryce N. 105–106
Harrison, President William Henry 22
Hartke, Senator Vance 73
Hay, Sec. of State John 73
Hayes, President Rutherford B. 46
Haynesworth, Judge Clement 119
Hickel, Sec. of Interior Walter 19
Hill-Burton Act 127
"Honeymoon" period of Presidents 125, 129, 170
Hoover, President Herbert C. 32
House Bypass Plan 160–161
Huitt, Ralph 42, 65–66
Huston Plan 151
Hyman, Sidney 51
Hyneman, Charles 133

Impeachment 22, 116–118, 147–165; Richard Nixon 13, 15, 26, 56; Andrew Johnson 25–26, 156, 157; House Judiciary Committee 151, 153–160; William O. Douglas 152
"imperial presidency" xii, 4–5, 6
impoundment xi, 10–11, 12, 110, 113–115
Independent Prosecutor 124, 145–146
Inherent powers 69–70
Interstate Commerce Act 28

Jackson, President Andrew vii, 21–22, 48
Javits, Senator Jacob 55, 143, 145, 149
Jaworski, Special Watergate Prosecutor Leon 116, 145, 158, 170
Jay, John 20, 71
Jefferson, President Thomas 21, 57, 67, 71, 83, 113
Johnson, President Andrew 13, 25–26, 156–157
Johnson, President Lyndon B. x, 1, 39, 48, 60–61, 74, 84–86, 99, 123, 127–128, 130
Joint resolution 74
Judiciary Act of 1789 20
Judiciary Committee, House of Representatives 13–15, 151, 153–160

Index

Kefauver, Senator Estes   133, 140
Kennedy, President John F.   1, 5, 10, 48, 53, 63, 74, 81, 91, 104, 112, 127, 130–131
"King Caucus"   21, 45
Kissinger, Henry   13;   and Vietnam   2, 10
Koenig, Louis   7
Korean War   6
Korematsu v. *United States*   88

Laotian War   3
Leadership, theories of   43–45
Legislative dominance theory   44
Legislative Reorganization Act   115
Legislative success score   61–63;   legislative machinery   107–111
Lincoln, President Abraham   23–25, 38, 53;   Lincoln-type President   48, 87
Lobbying, White House   104, 107
Locke, John   16–17, 56–57

Madison, James—Separation of Powers   8–9, 16, 19, 21, 45–47, 57, 71, 83–84, 154
Mansfield, Senator Mike   128
Marbury v. *Madison*   14, 117
Mathias, Senator Charles   88, 168, 173
McKinley, President William   29
McMahon, Senator Brien   xii, 64
Mills, Rep. Wilbur   113, 163
Monarch, the President as   4–5
Mondale, Sen. Walter F.   120, 133, 171
Monroe, President James   21
Montesquieu   57
Morris, Gouverneur   17–18
Morris, Robert   120

National emergencies   49, 87–88, 168–169, 172–173
National Security Council   36, 60, 89
Neustadt, Richard   52–53, 58, 89–90, 99
New Deal   ix
New Jersey Plan   17, 131
Nixon, President Richard M.   x–xii, 3–4, 11, 13–15, 25, 41–42, 48, 54–56, 58, 60, 81, 85–86, 88, 91, 102–104, 119–121, 123, 125, 147–165, 166, 168–172; and 93rd Congress, 1;   State of union message   1;   concept of executive branch management   1–2;   Public opinion ratings   1–2
Norris, Senator George   xii

O'Brien, Lawrence F.   105–106
Office of Consumer Affairs   37
Office of Management and Budget   2, 12, 102, 108–109, 113, 120, 123, 143, 167
Oversight, Congressional   118–120, 142–143

Parliamentary System   126, 131–133, 141–142
Pardon of President Nixon   170–172, 173
Patronage   34, 39, 53, 100–101
Pendleton, Rep. George   133
Pentagon Papers   120, 151
Percy, Senator Charles   150
"Plumbers"   3, 11
Political Parties   126–128, 141
Polk, President James K.   2, 23, 84
Polls   2, 8, 10, 94–95, 128, 130, 164–165, 170
Presidential messages   31, 34, 103–104
Presidential transition see Transition, Presidential
Presidentialists   5–9, 40–42

Rayburn, Speaker Sam   39, 127
Reed, Speaker Thomas B.   33, 39
Reedy, George   4
Reform Proposals   133–145; Finer, Herman (reform proposals)   135, 142; Hardin, Charles (reform proposal)   137–139; 141–142; Hyneman, Charles S. (reform proposal)   133; Kefauver, Sen. Estes (reform proposal)   133, 140; Mondale, Sen. Walter F. (reform proposal)   133; Pendleton, Rep. George (reform proposal)   133; Sundquist, James L.   136–137; Reuss, Rep. Henry (reform proposal)   135–136
Removal powers   19
Reorganization of Executive Branch   1, 2
Resignation, President Richard M. Nixon   160–163
Reuss, Rep. Henry   135, 136
Ribicoff, Abraham   54
Richard M. Nixon v. *United States* (see *United States* v. *Richard M. Nixon*)   116–117
Richardson, Attorney General Elliot   13, 119, 156
Rodino, Rep. Peter   159, 172
Roosevelt, President Franklin D.   32–35, 38, 50, 52–53, 58, 61, 87–89, 101, 129
Roosevelt, President Theodore   ix, 29–31, 48–50, 75
Rossiter, Clinton   41
Ruckelshaus, William   13, 119

"Saturday night massacre"   156, 171
Schlesinger, Arthur M., Jr.   6–7, 59

Index

Seiberling, Rep. John 169
Senate Special Committee on Termination of National Emergency 88, 172–173
Separation of Powers 16–17, 57–58, 65–66, 142–145
Sirica, Judge John J. 11
Southeast Asian Treaty Organization (SEATO) 86
Stanton, Secretary of War Edwin M. 24
State of the Union Address 1, 97, 103–104
St. Clair, James D. 116–117, 157–158
Stennis, Senator John 92–93
Strauss, Lewis 118
Sundquist, James L. 136–137
Sutherland, Justice George 71
Symington, Senator Stuart 79

Taft, President and Chief Justice William Howard 29, 47–48
Tennessee Valley Authority xii, 101
Tenure of Office Act 25, 26
Transition, Presidential 160–165, 170–172
Treaties 38, 70–80, 86
Truman, President Harry S 1, 43, 48, 50, 52, 67, 75, 86–87, 93, 113, 121–122, 127–128; Truman Doctrine 60–61, 162
Tugwell, Rexford 87
Turkey, aid to 172
Twenty-fifth Amendment 162–164
Twenty-second Amendment 26
Tyler, President John 22, 45, 74

United States v. *Belmont* 76
United States v. *Curtiss-Wright Export Corporation* 67, 69, 71
United States v. *Richard M. Nixon* (see *Richard M. Nixon* v. *United States*) 116–117, 144, 158

Vandenberg, Senator Arthur 72
Vetoes Grover Cleveland 18, 27; Franklin D. Roosevelt 34, 50, 58, 97–99; legislative veto 63, 123–124
Vietnam War 2, 84–86, 91–93; Nixon xi, 149; effect on presidency 7–8; L. B. Johnson 7, 8; and Congress 9–10, 55, 60; Tonkin Gulf Resolution 74, 82, 92–93, 128, 149
Virginia Plan 17, 131

Wade-Davis Bill 24
War-Making 81–93, 142; Presidential Interventionism 85–87; Congressional Curbs on 91–93; Public Opinion and 94–95
War Powers Act of 1973 12, 81, 92, 95, 124, 129, 149, 166–168

Washington, President George   vii, 18–20, 40, 51, 70
Watergate   64; "plumbers"   x, 11
Watergate   viii, 56, 121–123;   Senate Watergate Committee   x, 3;   Impact on Presidency   11–15, 144, 147–165;   Lessons of   169
Webster, Senator Daniel   21, 39
Whig Party   vii
Whig view of presidency   22, 47–48
White, Leonard   28
Wildarsky, Aaron   59
Wilson, President Woodrow   26, 30–31, 34, 43, 72–73, 87, 103, 121

Yom Kippur War   81;   Arab-Israeli War   4, 129
Young, Senator Milton   164

NOTES

NOTES